For Sophie and Louis. I love you to bits and pieces.
To my husband John, I could not have done this without your support,
encouragement and belief in me. Thank you. And for GiGi, whose imminent arrival
was the ultimate incentive to finish my book. Welcome to our family.

A huge thankyou to my parents Michael and Jan, sister Caitlin and John's parents Réne and
Wendy for all the countless hours of babysitting and help that made this possible.
To my amazing friends Amber and Claire for keeping me on track and always believing in me.
To all the babies who tested my food and to those who lent themselves for the photos, thank you.
To my creative and production teams; Guy, Mish, Rachel, Bianca, Vanessa and Belinda, I could
not have made this a reality without the help and expertise of you all. And a special thanks to Mish
for allowing us to shoot all the photos in her house – amazing!

A PLUM BOOK

Published in 2014 by
Pan Macmillan Australia Pty Limited
Level 25, 1 Market Street,
Sydney, NSW 2000, Australia

Level 1, 15–19 Claremont Street
South Yarra, Victoria 3141, Australia

First published in 2012 by Emily Dupuche

Text © 2012 Emily Dupuche
Photography © 2012 Guy Lavoipierre

The moral right of the author has been asserted.
A CIP catalogue record for this book is available from the National Library of Australia.

www.foodbabieslove.com.au

Food styling Mish Lilley (www.mishdelish.com)
Cover styling Rachel Vigor (www.rachelvigor.com)
Photography Guy Lavoipierre (www.guy.mu)
Design Vanessa Russell (www.raspberrycreative.com.au)
Editor Belinda Glindemann (www.bellepr.com)
Production Bianca Shugg (Jumpin Publishing)
Printing by 1010 Printing International Limited

food baby love

A guide to introducing your baby to solids

EMILY DUPUCHE

plum   Pan Macmillan Australia

contents...

The age appropriateness of recipes in this book is a guide only and will
vary depending on your baby's age when you first started them on solids.
Please check with your local child health centre or GP for the latest
guidelines on introducing solids if you have any questions or concerns.

hello

The recipes and anecdotes in this book will help guide and support you through the important process of introducing solids to your baby with practical advice and inspiration.

It's a big job — it can be fun and it can also be overwhelming at times. But it should be rewarding, watching your baby grow and develop, discovering the wonderful world of food.

I have three children — twins Sophie and Louis and their little sister, GiGi — and together we've spent a lot of time in the kitchen preparing and eating meals. I don't profess to know everything about introducing your baby to solids but I do know that, for a foodie, I was amazed at how nervous I was getting started. I also found it disconcerting when our progress didn't seem to match up with others, or where the experts said we should be. It was a relief to discover these nerves are common among all parents, and it made me realise that there is a need for some practical help to guide parents through the process of introducing solids.

Every baby is different and there really are few rights or wrongs with this. It's about finding your way, as best you can, and discovering what works for you and your baby.

So here I share with you some of my recipes that our family loved, for you to explore and enjoy, and some practical tips and advice to guide you along your way.

Here's to happy mealtimes, and a lifetime of food enjoyment.

Emily xx

getting ready for solids

Starting on solids is a major milestone in your baby's development. It's an exciting time and your kitchen will never look the same again. Say goodbye to bottles and sterilisers and hello to highchairs and colourful eating implements.

Starting on solids is something all mums and dads look forward to and no doubt will be the topic of much discussion among your parents' group. There is plenty of information available to you through your local child health centre, but here are some key points:

- Babies usually start on solids at 4–6 months of age (follow your instincts and signs your baby is giving you). Be guided by your health professional if you are unsure.

- Signs include: baby watching you when you eat, reaching out for your food, finding it harder to last between milk feeds and waking in the night looking for an extra feed.

- Get yourself ready. Buy a highchair, good quality plastic bib, plastic bowls and spoons and a box of organic

baby rice cereal from your supermarket.

- There is no specific order of foods to follow. You can start on rice cereal or vegetable purees or a combination of both. A suggested guide to getting started can be found on page 17.

- If your baby does not seem ready and fusses a lot when you first start on solids you may need to wait a bit longer before trying again. Consult your health professional on this.

- Plan to start solids when both parents can be home (e.g. Saturday lunch). Watching your baby take his or her first mouthfuls is pretty special so try to make sure you are both present with your camera charged and ready!

equipment and handy hints

Like just about any job, having the right equipment makes life easier. At first, this might seem like over-kill but once you really get into three meals a day and your baby is self-feeding, it will start to make sense and you'll be thankful for the early recommendation.

PREPARATION AND STORAGE

Stick blender A must! You will use this more than you could have imagined. From early purees to soups to delicious fruit smoothies, your stick blender will be out every day.

A good peeler Believe it or not, some are better than others and I cannot stress highly enough the importance of a good peeler. You will find yourself peeling more than ever and to have an efficient peeler will save you both time and frustration. Some can even peel tomatoes and pumpkins. These are ace and can be found at quality kitchenware stores — look for a serrated edge on at least one side and a blade that swivels.

Grater Again, consider this carefully as you will be grating veggies and cheese a lot. You want it to grate the food and not your fingers, you don't want it to be rusty, and ideally you want it to work well quickly. Again, some are better than others so have a look around.

A small saucepan and frying pan This may seem like an odd recommendation but you will be cooking much smaller portions than you are used to and having the right sized pot or pan for the job will not only reduce washing up, but will also help avoid your baby's food taking on a burnt flavour. Excess surface areas on hot pans can very quickly start to burn, which can affect flavour and be pretty tough to clean.

Whisks I have found it useful having a couple of sizes. I've always had a big one, but now that I often find myself whisking small quantities it is handy having a small one too.

Microwave steam jug, with lid I use mine all the time. I never thought I would as I've never really been into microwave cooking, but I was given one and now it's probably one of my favourite things. From steaming veggies to stewing fruits, it's become a kitchen staple. I was forever getting distracted and burning pots of stewing fruit on the stovetop (I even destroyed a couple of pots full of bottles and pump attachments — melting plastic and burnt pots stink!). I blame it on sleep deprivation.

Ice cube trays Cubes of baby food are a godsend. When you have a freezer full of snap-lock bags loaded and labelled with baby meals you will feel like Super Parent, and deservedly so. You will be cubing food for many months, so invest in a set of appropriately sized trays with lids. The lid will help keep out ice burn and stop the food absorbing freezer odours. They will also help you to manage your available space as you can stack trays more effectively. There are many brands available at baby supply stores.

Storage containers As your baby progresses to eating full-size meals (about five cubes or ½ cup of food) you might find it easier to start freezing complete portions rather than cubes, so a set of good food tubs with sturdy lids will come in handy. Consider the shape (round tubs are not space efficient) and you will want to label them; use a removable sticker or buy containers with erasable label tabs. Sheets of printer labels from office supply stores are perfect.

Measuring cups and spoons Nothing special required here, just a set of interlocking metric cup and spoon measures. A range of glass or plastic measuring jugs will also come in handy, but are not essential.

Food processor/chopper Adding this to my essentials list was a bit of an afterthought but they are super handy for all manner of things and great for making veggies invisible. There are many types available so get one that suits your budget and your kitchen storage.

Scales Where possible I have tried to provide measurements other than weight, but sometimes weight is the best option so a set of scales is always handy.

SITTING DOWN TO EAT

Highchair This will be a permanent fixture in your kitchen/ dining room for a good couple of years so choose one you can bear to look at, that fits in the space you have available and, importantly, is easy to clean. Beware of lots of padding. You can spend a small fortune on one with all the bells and whistles but this is not necessary. This is one instance where you can afford to spend a little less. A note on sitting up: many babies are not able to sit unsupported when they start solids. Don't let this impede you. You can use a bouncer-type chair or babies can be easily propped up with towels in a highchair, which I think is best as it gets your baby used to the structure of mealtime.

Bibs Get a good-quality dishwasher-safe plastic bib with an open food-catcher tray. Some are a bit floppy and don't effectively catch the spills, and fabric ones do little to protect the clothing underneath from wetness and stickiness. The earlier you start using a bib, the less likely your baby is to resist wearing one.

Bowls You don't need many (we only have one each) but you do need good quality. Believe it or not, the design of the bowl does make a difference to your baby's ability to master self-feeding. Look for those with an internal edge that allows your baby to get some leverage. In my experience this is far more beneficial than suction bases or lids. It is important to use different bowls for heating and serving to ensure the bowl put in front of your baby is not hot.

Spoons Always use plastic spoons and never metal. Metal spoons can get hot and accidentally burn your baby. There are countless options available and you may want to test a couple based on your baby's eating style, but in the early days when you are doing the spooning, just a simple straight spoon is more than adequate. Watch the scoop size – some are too big to easily fit in a young baby's mouth. I used readily available supermarket spoons at first and then progressed to the larger ones when the kids took over the feeding role (the larger scoop helps to keep more on the wobbly spoon!).

Face washers This eating is a messy business. Choose lovely lightweight face washers that are soft on your baby's face and don't hold food in their fibres. Having one to wave in the air can also work well to help early eaters look up, giving you better access to their mouths.

Drop sheet A simple calico drop sheet spread out under the highchair at each meal has saved me countless hours of wiping, mopping and vacuuming the floor. I know, because it took me many months to cotton on to this device. Simply wipe down the chair, fold in the sheet and take it outside and shake. Throw it in the machine every couple of days and you can avoid getting on your hands and knees after each meal. Get a couple of these or use an old bed sheet. You can buy calico at fabric stores or painting drop sheets at hardware stores.

Smocks I cannot recommend these highly enough. I'm sure you are now thinking I am a cleanliness nut, but I'm not. I'm just practical. Using a smock means that outfits survive the meal unscathed, especially the sleeves and laps which are unprotected by bibs, so you don't have to change your baby's clothes after each meal.

---

products I recommend

- Bellamy's Organic Baby Rice Cereal and Organic Baby Porridge: Quality Australian-made products that are readily available.
- Ice cube trays: Check out an Aussie product called Qubies (www.qubies.com). They save you laboriously spooning small amounts of food into separate ice cube tray holes and it's super easy to remove the cubes.
- Highchair: Ikea's Antilop plastic highchair is cheap, functional and easy to clean (www.ikea.com).
- Bibs and bowls: Check out the range from Baby Bjorn (www.babybjorn.com).

freezing and reheating food

Although older babies are not reliant on a sterile environment, a few good food hygiene rules should be followed when preparing and serving meals. And yes, you can stop sterilising bottles now. Hooray!

First, always wash your hands thoroughly before cooking and preparing your baby's meals. Also follow general safe food preparation rules such as not chopping veggies where raw meat has been prepared.

Freezing

- Cool food as fast as possible and get it straight into the freezer. Don't leave it in the fridge for ages before freezing.

- Ensure ice cube trays are well sealed to avoid odour transfer and ice burn.

- Once cubes are frozen, pop them out of their trays and store them in snap-lock bags. Label them clearly, including the date you cooked the meal and/or an expiry date (no more than six weeks is a good rule of thumb).

- Never refreeze leftovers.

Heating

- It's OK to thaw in the fridge, a saucepan or a microwave.

- Always ensure food is heated through thoroughly and then allowed to cool before giving it to your baby.

- Stir food well to ensure there are no hot spots.

- Do not save leftovers from one meal to serve at the next, especially meat. Babies are still sensitive to the bacteria that can form in dodgy food handling practices.

- One of the many benefits of freezing food in cubes is that you can thaw one or two cubes at a time in the microwave and quickly prepare more if your baby is hungry, minimising waste and giving you peace of mind.

A note on allergies

Food allergies in young babies are not uncommon and some are more serious than others. Official guidelines now recommend introducing allergenic foods in the first year of a child's life, even for infants at high risk of allergy. Always consult your health professional for the latest information and advice, especially if you have a family history of allergies.

You must proceed with caution and watch for any signs of change or distress in your baby, such as redness in the face, hives, vomiting, diarrhoea, eczema, or trouble breathing.

Common foods that are known allergens include:

- Eggs
- Nuts
- Dairy
- Soy
- Wheat
- Fish and shellfish

Acidic foods

As babies are such sensitive little souls, they can sometimes have a reaction to acidic foods. This is not an allergy as such, but can cause a sensitive bottom. Strawberries and tomatoes are common culprits. If this occurs, simply avoid these foods until your bub is a bit older.

the humble herb

Please try to use fresh herbs in your baby's cooking. Not only do they add a variety of health benefits, but they can also lift a meal to a new level of flavour and freshness. A sprinkling of fresh chopped parsley on just about any meal adds zing and good looks to your creation. Using fresh herbs as a garnish will also help your baby's palate develop. Your baby will enjoy a wider variety of tastes and colours and become used to the colour green on their plate.

Seasonality We all know that foods taste best when they are in season. They are also likely to be fresher, spending less time in long storage losing nutrients and, conveniently, they are cheaper. The in-season fruit and veggies available to you will vary depending on when your baby was born. If you're introducing solids in summer, you have the advantage of a plethora of fresh fruit such as sweet mangoes, berries and stone fruits. If you are cooking in the cooler months, you can stew winter fruits like apples, pears and rhubarb. You can also try custard apple, and don't forget the brilliance of frozen fruits such as berries and mango cheeks from your supermarket. These are picked and packed in peak season and are a great alternative to fresh fruits.

the first few weeks

the first few weeks

I hope I never forget the day my babies first tried solids. For Sophie, the exertion of a couple of spoons of rice cereal had her falling asleep in the highchair. And Louis, perhaps not as ready as Sophie but not one to be left behind, was all bib. He didn't eat much. Priceless memories!

The first few days of tasting food will be very strange for your baby. Be very encouraging and always smile as you are feeding. You will see some funny faces and tongue thrusting. It's not that babies don't like it, they just don't know what to do. Don't expect them to attempt more than a couple of spoonfuls of rice cereal and even then they will probably spit it out. It's just to introduce them to texture in their mouth.

Try to structure your baby's meal just before a sleep – it's exhausting work. Do not offer solids when your baby is hungry. Either follow a normal milk feed with solids or adopt a split-feed routine whereby you offer half milk/ solids/half milk (many of us have a sanity-saving sleep routine we are following so it's best to stick with advice regarding feed times). Remember that their regular milk remains the main source of nutrition for babies for many months to come; the introduction of solids is just about exposing babies to as many tastes, textures and colours as possible. They will decide how much they want to eat so don't stress about quantities, just ensure their milk volumes remain consistent.

Start with your chosen first food (I recommend iron-fortified rice cereal or a veggie puree) mixed with your baby's regular milk – either breast or formula. You can also use cooled boiled water, but the familiar taste of milk will help them along. You want it to be quite runny, about the consistency of pouring cream. If it's too thick or pasty it will clag up in their mouths making it difficult to swallow. You will find it's slow going feeding your baby and the mixture will thicken up pretty quickly, so keep an eye on the consistency, adding more liquid as required. At first offer your baby your chosen first food once a day for four or five days, then start to introduce some new foods. There is no specific order of foods to follow, although I do recommend offering fruit purees after you've tried a few veggie ones, so your baby doesn't develop a sweet tooth.

Don't despair. Have patience. If you think your baby doesn't like a particular food, don't give up and move to the next food – see the three days out to help them develop a taste for it. Remember, it can take up to 10 attempts at presenting a food for your baby to enjoy it.

at a glance

- Try to serve meals just before a sleep.
- Be very encouraging and always smile as you are feeding your baby.
- Do not offer solids when your baby is hungry – follow on from their normal milk or adopt a 'split-feed' routine.
- Start on rice cereal or vegetable purees or a combination of both.
- There is no specific order of foods to follow, and you can mix first foods together.
- Don't despair! It can take up to 10 attempts at presenting a food for a baby to enjoy it.

here is a guide

Start with very small portions – about 1 teaspoon of your chosen first food blended with a little of your baby's regular milk. Increase by 1 teaspoon per day until you reach about 1 tablespoon (about 4–5 days). First foods can include any of the options listed below on their own or as a blend.

When your baby has mastered eating off a spoon and is consuming about 1 tablespoon at a sitting, you can then introduce a second daily meal. Gradually increase the quantity to 2–4 tablespoons (or cubes) per meal and build up to three meals a day at your baby's own pace. Use the quantities below as a guide only as every baby's appetite is different – they will tell you when they have had enough by turning their head away or arching their back.

		breakfast	lunch	dinner
	day 1		1 tsp chosen first food blended with your baby's regular milk	
	day 2		2 tsp chosen first food blended with your baby's regular milk	
	day 3		3 tsp chosen first food blended with your baby's regular milk	
	day 4		4 tsp (1 tbs) chosen first food blended with your baby's regular milk	2 tsp chosen first food blended with your baby's regular milk
	day 5		2 cubes carrot puree or veggie mix blended with your baby's regular milk	1–2 cubes carrot puree or veggie mix blended with your baby's regular milk
	day 6		3 cubes carrot puree or veggie mix blended with your baby's regular milk	2–3 cubes carrot puree or veggie mix blended with your baby's regular milk
	day 7		3–4 cubes carrot puree or veggie mix blended with your baby's regular milk	2–3 cubes carrot puree or veggie mix blended with your baby's regular milk
	day 8		3–4 cubes sweet potato puree or veggie mix blended with your baby's regular milk	3–4 cubes sweet potato puree or veggie mix blended with your baby's regular milk
	day 9		3–4 cubes sweet potato puree or veggie mix blended with your baby's regular milk	3–4 cubes sweet potato puree or veggie mix blended with your baby's regular milk
	day 10		3–4 cubes sweet potato puree or veggie mix blended with your baby's regular milk	3–4 cubes sweet potato puree or veggie mix blended with your baby's regular milk
	day 11		3–4 cubes zucchini puree or veggie mix blended with your baby's regular milk	3–4 cubes zucchini puree or veggie mix blended with your baby's regular milk

		breakfast	lunch	dinner
	day 12		3–4 cubes zucchini puree or veggie mix blended with your baby's regular milk	3–4 cubes zucchini puree or veggie mix blended with your baby's regular milk
	day 13		3–4 cubes zucchini puree or veggie mix blended with your baby's regular milk	3–4 cubes zucchini puree or veggie mix blended with your baby's regular milk
	day 14	2 tsp rice cereal or baby porridge	3–4 cubes apple puree or fruit and veggie mix blended with your baby's regular milk	3–4 cubes apple puree or fruit and veggie mix blended with your baby's regular milk
	day 15	2 tsp rice cereal or baby porridge	3–4 cubes apple puree or fruit and veggie mix blended with your baby's regular milk	3–4 cubes apple puree or fruit and veggie mix blended with your baby's regular milk
	day 16	2 tsp rice cereal or baby porridge	3–4 cubes apple puree or fruit and veggie mix blended with your baby's regular milk	3–4 cubes apple puree or fruit and veggie mix blended with your baby's regular milk
	day 17	3 tsp baby porridge	4–5 cubes pumpkin-based veggie mix blended with your baby's regular milk	4–5 cubes pumpkin-based veggie mix blended with your baby's regular milk
	day 18	3 tsp baby porridge	4–5 cubes pumpkin-based veggie mix blended with your baby's regular milk	4–5 cubes pumpkin-based veggie mix blended with your baby's regular milk
	day 19	3 tsp baby porridge	4–5 cubes pumpkin-based veggie mix blended with your baby's regular milk	4–5 cubes pumpkin-based veggie mix blended with your baby's regular milk
	day 20	4 tsp baby porridge	4–5 cubes broccoli- or cauliflower-based veggie mix blended with your baby's regular milk	4–5 cubes broccoli- or cauliflower-based veggie mix blended with your baby's regular milk
	day 21	4 tsp baby porridge	4–5 cubes broccoli- or cauliflower-based veggie mix blended with your baby's regular milk	4–5 cubes broccoli- or cauliflower-based veggie mix blended with your baby's regular milk
	day 22	4 tsp baby porridge	4–5 cubes broccoli- or cauliflower-based veggie mix blended with your baby's regular milk	4–5 cubes broccoli- or cauliflower-based veggie mix blended with your baby's regular milk

- Be sure to vary the vegetable blends you offer your baby, to ensure a wide variety of colours and flavours.
- Rice cereal can cause constipation in some babies. If this happens, speak with your health professional and remember that certain fruits can help, such as pear. A little pear puree mixed with the rice cereal should do the trick.
- It's best to introduce veggie purees before fruit to avoid your baby relying on the natural sweetness of fruit. Too much fruit early on can lead to a sweet tooth, making it harder to introduce other foods. Of course some fruits are fine but try not to rely on them to get a meal eaten.
- It's OK if your baby isn't eating great volumes as this phase is all about tastes and textures, not nutrition.

volume guide

A guide to quantities using ice cube trays:

1 teaspoon = 5 ml

1 tablespoon = 20 ml (so, 4 tsp = 1 tbs)

1 cube = 20–25 ml depending on the brand of ice cube tray (about 1 tbs)

1 cup = 250 ml

10 cubes = 1 cup (approx.)

milk feeds and other drinks

Breast milk or formula will remain the most important source of nutrition for your baby until the age of one, even though solid food will gradually replace some milk feeds.

As your baby progresses on solids you will start to reduce milk feeds, but you will need to ensure that total milk intake remains about 500–600 ml a day (breast milk or formula). You can help supplement this by using lots of dairy in your cooking such as white sauce, yoghurt and cheese. Lots of my recipes contain dairy and these combined with a hearty breakfast will help meet your target.

Once babies start on solids they can also start to enjoy drinks other than milk. Tap water with fluoride should be your first choice: it's freely available and won't add to tooth decay or cause sticky spills. And it's the best at counteracting any constipation issues.

Always offer a drink with your baby's meal, from a cup or beaker. While it is OK for your baby to have well-diluted fruit juice, I see no need to look beyond water. It is the best accompaniment to a meal and it won't take the edge off your baby's hunger in the same way milk or juice would. Also, juices add to sugar intake, increasing the chances of developing a sweet tooth.

Do not offer cow's milk as a drink before your baby is about 12 months. While it is OK to cook with, breast milk or formula should remain your baby's milk drink until then. Other dairy foods such as butter, cheese and yoghurt are fine to introduce once you have gone through the basic puree introduction.

first purees

Here we go...you're off and racing. Get your ice cube trays out and have your veggie peeler handy. Happy steaming, happy mashing!

I've always been very happy and comfortable in the kitchen, so I was surprised by just how nervous I felt the first time I had to prepare carrot puree for Sophie and Louis. I've since discovered that these feelings are not uncommon among new parents. While it is strangely comforting to know I'm not alone, it begs the question, why? It must be something to do with our parental instincts and our desire to always do right by our little ones.

Purees are not hard. In fact, they're nearly impossible to get wrong. All of the purees in this chapter are suitable for freezing and each recipe will make about 1 cup (250 ml) or 10 cubes.

These cubes will become fantastic veggie bases for you to add to meals over the next couple of months, allowing you to create your own flavour combinations.

Note: Quantities provided are just guides. Once you get underway, cook as much of each vegetable as you have on hand and use them to add to different meals. Cooking times will vary depending on the size of your diced veggies.

carrot

Age: first month of eating

Suitable for freezing

Makes: about 1 cup

250 g carrot (about 2 carrots), peeled and diced into 1.5 cm pieces

Place the carrot in a small saucepan with a tight-fitting lid and barely cover with water. Cook over low heat for 12–15 minutes or until soft. Strain, reserving a little of the cooking liquid.

Alternatively, place the carrot in the top of a double steamer and steam for 15 minutes or until tender. If you have a microwave-safe cooking dish with a lid, place the carrot and ½ cup of water in the dish, cover and microwave on high for 5 minutes or until soft. Strain as necessary, reserving the cooking liquid.

Use a stick blender to puree the carrot, adding a little of the cooking water to help thin it down and make it smooth.

Set aside 2 teaspoons of pureed carrot for your baby's meal and freeze the remaining puree in an ice cube tray.

sweet potato

Age: first month of eating

Suitable for freezing

Makes: about 1 cup

250 g sweet potato (about ½ a sweet potato), peeled and diced into rough 1 cm pieces

Place the sweet potato in a small saucepan with a tight-fitting lid and barely cover with water. Cover and cook over low heat for 15 minutes or until soft. Strain, reserving a little of the cooking liquid.

Alternatively, place the sweet potato in the top of a double steamer and steam for 15–20 minutes or until tender. If you have a microwave-safe cooking dish with a lid, place the sweet potato and 50 ml of water in the dish, cover and microwave on high for 5 minutes or until soft. Strain as necessary, reserving the cooking liquid.

Use a stick blender to puree the sweet potato, adding a little of the cooking water to help thin it down and make it smooth.

Set aside 2 teaspoons of pureed sweet potato for your baby's meal and freeze the remaining puree in an ice cube tray.

> *tip* Try lightly roasting cubes of sweet potato for about 20 minutes at 180°C. Add a very light sprinkling of cinnamon and puree. Delicious!

broccoli

Age: first month of eating

Suitable for freezing

Makes: about 1 cup

250 g head of broccoli, trimmed and cut into florets

Place the broccoli pieces in a small saucepan with a tight-fitting lid and barely cover the base with water. Cover and cook over low heat for 8–10 minutes or until the broccoli is tender and still bright green. Strain, reserving a little of the cooking liquid.

Alternatively, the place broccoli in the top of a double steamer and steam for 10 minutes or until tender. If you have a microwave-safe cooking dish with a lid, place the broccoli and 20 ml of water in the dish, cover and microwave on high for 3 minutes or until soft. Strain as necessary, reserving the cooking liquid.

Use a stick blender to puree the broccoli, adding a little of the cooking water to help thin it down and make it smooth.

Set aside 2 teaspoons of pureed broccoli for your baby's meal and freeze the remaining puree in an ice cube tray.

cauliflower

Age: first month of eating

Suitable for freezing

Makes: about 1 cup

250 g head of cauliflower, trimmed and cut into florets

Place the cauliflower pieces in a small saucepan with a tight-fitting lid and barely cover the base with water. Cover and cook over low heat for 8–10 minutes or until tender. Strain, reserving a little of the cooking liquid.

Alternatively, place the cauliflower in the top of a double steamer and steam for 10 minutes or until tender. If you have a microwave-safe cooking dish with a lid, place the cauliflower and 20 ml of water in the dish, cover and microwave on high for 3 minutes or until soft. Strain as necessary, reserving the cooking liquid.

Use a stick blender to puree the cauliflower, adding a little of the cooking water to help thin it down and make it smooth.

Set aside 2 teaspoons of pureed cauliflower for your baby's meal and freeze the remaining puree in an ice cube tray.

tip These two partners in crime are terrific on their own but perhaps even better when mixed together, as cauliflower can soften the strong flavour of broccoli. To prepare a blend, use half the quantity of each in the cooking process. I also very quickly started adding Cheesy Sauce (page 80) to this blend. This combination became a firm favourite added to just about anything but particularly the Aussie Beef Casserole (page 56) and Bolognaise for Little People (page 60) as tomato and cheese work so well together.

zucchini

Age: first month of eating

Suitable for freezing

Makes: about 1 cup

300 g zucchini (about 1 zucchini), diced

Place the zucchini in a small saucepan with a tight-fitting lid and barely cover with water. Cover and cook over low heat for 8–10 minutes or until soft. Strain, reserving a little of the cooking liquid.

Alternatively, place the zucchini in the top of a double steamer and steam for 10 minutes or until tender. If you have a microwave-safe cooking dish with a lid, place the zucchini and 30 ml of water in the dish, cover and microwave on high for 4 minutes or until soft. Strain as necessary, reserving the cooking liquid.

Use a stick blender to puree the zucchini.

Set aside 2 teaspoons of pureed zucchini for your baby's meal and freeze the remaining puree in an ice cube tray.

> *tip* Zucchini are naturally quite watery so you probably won't need to add any extra liquid when pureeing. The mild flavour of zucchini works well with carrots and added to pasta and rice dishes.

pumpkin

Age: first month of eating

Suitable for freezing

Makes: about 1 cup

200 g butternut pumpkin (about ¼ pumpkin), peeled, deseeded and roughly chopped

Place the pumpkin in a small saucepan with a tight-fitting lid and barely cover with water. Cover and cook over low heat for 8–10 minutes or until soft. Strain, reserving a little of the cooking liquid.

Alternatively, place the pumpkin in the top of a double steamer and steam for 10–12 minutes or until tender. If you have a microwave-safe cooking dish with a lid, place the pumpkin and 20 ml of water in the dish, cover and microwave on high for 3–5 minutes or until soft. Strain as necessary, reserving the cooking liquid.

Use a stick blender to puree the pumpkin, adding a little of the cooking water to help thin it down and make it smooth.

Set aside 2 teaspoons of pureed pumpkin for your baby's meal and freeze the remaining puree in an ice cube tray.

> *tip* Butternut pumpkins are readily available and have a reliably sweet flesh. They are also easier to cut and peel than other varieties. But of course you can use any pumpkin you like.

root veggies

Age: first month of eating

Suitable for freezing

Makes: about 1 cup

200 g root vegetables, peeled and roughly chopped (try parsnip, swede and turnip)

Place the vegetable pieces in a small saucepan with a tight-fitting lid and cover with water. Cover and cook over low heat for 15 minutes or until soft. Strain, reserving a little of the cooking liquid.

Alternatively, place the vegetables in the top of a double steamer and steam for 20 minutes or until tender. If you have a microwave-safe cooking dish with a lid, place the vegetables and 20 ml of water in the dish, cover and microwave on high for 4 minutes or until soft. Strain as necessary, reserving the cooking liquid.

Use a stick blender to puree the veggies, adding a little of the cooking water to help thin it down and make it smooth.

Set aside 2 teaspoons of pureed vegetables for your baby's meal and freeze the remaining puree in an ice cube tray.

peas

Age: first month of eating

Suitable for freezing

Makes: about 1 cup

1½ cups frozen peas

Place the peas in a small saucepan with a tight-fitting lid and barely cover with water. Cover and cook over low heat for 3–5 minutes or until the peas are tender and still bright green. Strain, reserving a little of the cooking liquid.

Alternatively, place the peas in a microwave-safe dish with a lid along with 20 ml water and microwave on high for 2 minutes.

Puree the peas using a food processor or blender on the fastest setting, adding a little of the cooking liquid to help make the puree smooth. Pass the puree through a sieve to remove excess husks.

Set aside 2 teaspoons of puree for your baby's meal and freeze the remaining puree in an ice cube tray.

> *tip* Enhance your pea puree for older babies by adding a clove of garlic to the cooking water. Remove the garlic before pureeing the peas. Adding a leaf or two of mint to the cooking water also works really well.

mashed potato

Age: first month of eating

Suitable for freezing

Makes: about 1 cup

250 g potato (about 1 potato), peeled and diced

Place the potato in a small saucepan and barely cover the base with water. Cook over low heat for 12–15 minutes or until tender. Strain, reserving a little of the cooking liquid. Or, if you have a microwave-safe cooking dish with a lid, place the potato and 50 ml of water in the dish, cover and microwave on high for 5 minutes or until soft. Strain as necessary, reserving the cooking liquid.

Mash the potato with a fork or potato masher, adding a little of the cooking water or your baby's regular milk to help thin down the mash and make it smooth. Do not use a stick blender as the glutens in potato break down under high stress and your mash will become like glue.

Set aside 2 teaspoons of mashed potato for your baby's meal and freeze the remaining mash in an ice cube tray.

> *tip* If you are concerned that your mash still has lumps, push it through a fine sieve with the back of a spoon. Also, remember that babies need fat so don't be afraid of using a little butter in your mashed potato once your baby has been eating solids for a few weeks.

cooked tomato

Age: first month of eating

Suitable for freezing

Makes: about 1 cup

2 medium–ripe tomatoes, peeled, deseeded and roughly chopped

1 tablespoon butter

Buttery tomato is a great addition to any vegetable puree, adding a whole new flavour dimension. Remember, where there is tomato, fresh parsley loves to follow!

Heat a saucepan over medium heat and melt the butter. When it starts to foam, add the chopped tomatoes and cook, stirring for about 5 minutes until the tomato becomes pulpy.

Remove from the heat and puree to the desired consistency. Allow to cool before dividing into portions. Use with any other vegetable puree or mix with rice cereal or plain boiled rice when your baby is experimenting with texture.

Freeze any remaining puree in an ice cube tray.

> *tip* A good veggie peeler will peel a tomato like an apple.

sweet corn

Age: first month of eating

Suitable for freezing

Makes: about ½ cup

2 cobs of sweet corn, outer leaves removed, or 150 g (1 cup) frozen corn kernels

If using fresh corn, place the cobs in a pot and cover with water. Bring to the boil, cover and simmer for 15 minutes. Remove the cobs and allow them to cool a little before removing the kernels with a sharp knife. Reserve the cooking water. For frozen corn, cook according to packet directions.

To puree, place the kernels in a blender or food processor with 50 ml of cooking water and blend on high speed for 2 minutes, or until smooth. Pass the puree through a fine sieve to remove any remaining corn husks.

Set aside a few teaspoons for your baby's meal and freeze any remaining puree in an ice cube tray.

tip Passing the corn through a sieve means you will lose some volume. This recipe will yield about ½ cup husk-free puree, so double the quantities if you'd like more.

pear

Age: first month of eating

Suitable for freezing

Makes: about 1 cup

2 ripe pears, peeled, cored and roughly chopped

Place the pears in a small saucepan with a sprinkling of water, cover and cook over low heat for 10 minutes or until soft.

If using a microwave, place the pears in a microwave-safe container with a tight-fitting lid and microwave on high for 5 minutes.

Puree the cooked pears using a stick blender. Set aside a few teaspoons for your baby's meal and freeze any remaining puree in an ice cube tray.

apple

Age: first month of eating

Suitable for freezing

Makes: about 1 cup

2 apples (Granny Smith are traditional cooking apples but not as sweet as others — feel free to use your favourite variety), peeled, cored and roughly chopped

Place the apples in a small saucepan with a sprinkling of water, cover and cook over low heat for 10 minutes or until soft.

If using a microwave, place the apples in a microwave-safe container with a tight-fitting lid and cook on high for 5–8 minutes (no water necessary).

Puree the cooked apples using a stick blender. Set aside a few teaspoons for your baby's meal and freeze the remaining puree in an ice cube tray.

tip Once you are underway with solids, puree 6 or 10 apples at a time. Apple puree freezes brilliantly and it's terrific to have on hand to add to just about anything from breakfast porridge to meaty stews.

banana

Age: first month of eating

Suitable for freezing

Makes: about 1 cup

½ ripe banana (not too ripe and certainly not under-ripe and chalky), peeled

Nature's power food. And a parent's best friend. Packed full of goodness, they even come in their own wrapper! Mashed banana is a great first food for babies but can cause constipation in some, so keep an eye on the nappy situation and cut down if required.

Mash the banana with a fork. Mix with a little of your baby's regular milk and a teaspoon of rice cereal.

avocado

Age: first month of eating

Suitable for freezing

Makes: about 1 cup

1 ripe avocado

Another brilliant food provided by Mother Nature. Make sure you don't use 'woody' avocados or ones with lots of brown patches, as these can have an unpleasant taste and texture. A simple rule: if you wouldn't eat it, then don't expect your baby to.

Start by cutting out a quarter (or a small wedge) of the avocado only, as once the flesh is removed from the stone it will oxidise quickly and turn brown.

Scoop out the flesh from the piece you are using and mash with a fork. Mix with a little of your baby's regular milk and a teaspoon of rice cereal.

> *tip* If your baby didn't take to the avocado and you have spare mashed avo in the fridge, try a squeeze of lemon juice, a dash of Tabasco sauce, some salt and pepper and, voila! You have a mini guacamole to enjoy over a glass of wine when your baby has gone to bed.

stone fruits

Age: first month of eating

Suitable for freezing

Makes: about 1 cup

4–6 fresh stone fruits, peeled and stones removed (try apricots, peaches or nectarines but choose one variety at a time)

Stone fruits are great pureed and added to meat dishes or plain yoghurts, or simply peel them as a terrific finger food for babies to suck on – sweet and sticky! Just make sure the fruit is ripe as you don't want any sourness to turn them off.

If using fresh fruit, simply puree with a stick blender.

For a cooked version, place the fruit in a small saucepan with a sprinkling of water, cover and cook over low heat for 10 minutes or until soft.

Alternatively, place the fruit in a microwave-safe container with a tight-fitting lid and microwave on high for 5 minutes.

Puree the cooked fruit using a stick blender. Set aside a few teaspoons for your baby's meal and freeze any remaining puree in an ice cube tray.

the next few months

the next few months

Now that you have introduced your baby to a range of basic fruit and veg, you can start to have some fun with cooking actual meals.

Introduce red and white meats, fish, lentils and other pulses – all good sources of protein – and start to experiment with texture. I followed the premise of nutrition first, meaning if my babies weren't coping with the texture I would simply puree the meal to ensure they had full tummies before heading off to bed. I really found they only started to deal with texture once they had opposing front teeth. I know it's different for every baby, but I was always striving for them to sleep through the night so wanted to get as much tucker into them as possible, and wasn't going to be let down by a lump or two! Like anything, don't give up. Keep trying with texture, as it's important they do get used to some lumps and bumps, but there's no need to rush it.

I found the best way to manage my babies' diet was to set a meal plan each week, create a shopping list and then have a cook-up. Once my freezer was stacked with little cubes of food we could relax into meals, easily adding an extra cube of this or that as their appetites and general inquisitiveness grew.

I can't stress enough the benefits of being prepared. When your baby starts grizzling with hunger you do not want to be caught short. Thinking about it all at the start of the week also allows you to ensure you are providing a range of flavours and meeting nutritional needs. It's pretty easy to get stuck in a rut and find yourself feeding your baby the same foods over and over, but it's in this early stage that you want to expose them to as many different foods as possible to try to avoid creating a fussy eater. Frozen cubes will give you endless flexibility to create a variety of meals for no extra effort on your part.

At about eight or nine months of age, your baby will show signs of wanting to use his or her own spoon. Encourage this. Remember the smock, the bib, the drop sheet? This is why. Have two spoons on hand – one for your baby to use and the other for you to actually feed your bub. This will encourage independence and help them to increase their enjoyment of food. You will find it liberating when you don't actually have to sit there feeding your baby every spoonful. But like anything, if it takes your baby longer to exert their feeding independence don't panic, they will get there in their own time.

breakfast, lunch and dinner

By about 6–8 months (depending on when you started introducing solids) your baby will probably be on three meals a day, each of about ½ to 1 cup in volume – somewhere between 5 and 10 cubes.

Lunch should be the main meal of the day for your baby because eating a meal should be enjoyable for everyone – and as parents of young babies we know that they typically get tired, cranky and generally over it by about 4 pm. So allow your baby to enjoy a main meal before their lunchtime sleep and offer them a light, easy-to-eat dinner that won't cause too much consternation. I always tried to limit offering new foods or challenging them with finger food at night in case it tipped one of them over the edge and into a meltdown.

Breakfast A wholegrain cereal, fruit puree and full-fat yoghurt is best, followed by toast (with Vegemite, of course) cut into small pieces, which is a good way to introduce babies to finger foods.

Lunch The main meal. Make it protein-based by using either meat, fish, pulses or tofu.

Dinner Play it safe. Thick veggie soups with buttered toast are a great way to top up your baby's daily veggie intake and they are so easy to consume.

Snacks Afternoon tea will become a bit of a fixture, especially once they drop that milk feed at around 12 months of age. Fruit and yoghurt are a good way to keep up dairy intake and commercially available plain biscuits are the ultimate convenience. (Cruskits are terrific as they dissolve in the mouth and don't require teeth!)

Fats, proteins and iron

Your baby needs fat. If you use 'lite' products for yourself then please buy the full-fat equivalent for your baby. Babies should not have any low-fat versions of cheese, yoghurt or milk. Always use butter and not margarine – butter is less processed and contains the essential fats their growing bodies need.

Protein builds healthy bones and tissue and is vital for the growth and development of all children. Protein is also filling, so if your baby is still waking at night for a milk feed, chances are that they are not getting adequate protein during the day.

Iron is crucial in promoting healthy growth and development. Try to give your baby a variety of iron-rich foods, such as meat, lentils and leafy green veggies.

breakfast

Of all the meals, breakfast is the most predictable, but that's OK. After all, isn't it for you too? It's also a great way to load up on dairy. You are looking to provide 500–600 ml a day, so milk and yoghurt in a breakfast cereal are great contributors to meeting this target.

Cereals At some point in this phase you will be able to migrate from baby porridge to real oats. There is no set time, just whenever you next need to replenish your supplies. Oats are much cheaper to buy than baby porridge, but do take a little longer to prepare. I suggest you opt for instant oats, which are much quicker to make than traditional oats. But either is fine.

In the main, stay away from well-known commercial breakfast cereals, especially those marketed at kids, as these tend to be high in sugar and salt and low in goodness, despite what it says on the box. However, wholegrain breakfast biscuits such as Vita Brits and OatBrits are fine to use.

Toast Always try to use a quality wholemeal or multigrain bread. White processed bread has little nutritional value and should be avoided. I have never once found the grains to be an issue – in fact, some of the super-seedy breads available are my children's favourites as they have such depth of flavour. Oh, and I know for sure they are acting as a terrific source of fibre.

Vegemite, jam and peanut butter are good toppings but never honey, as there is a risk of infant botulism. You must make sure you are vigilant the first time your baby tries peanut butter in case of the dreaded nut allergy. If there is a family history of nut allergies, consult your health professional before trying it out on your baby. While jam may be made from fruit, it is also very sweet and sugary. Many of us try to limit our babies' sugar intake for as long as possible for fear they will develop a sweet tooth, so be mindful of this if jam is a favourite in your home. Vegemite and its derivative Cheesybite are great, safe choices. So is cream cheese.

Frustratingly, you will probably find your baby nibbles and licks the toast rather than eats it. Just start with a quarter of a piece and work your way up. If all else fails, pop it in a container and give it to them at morning or afternoon tea. Babies aren't as discriminating as us and don't mind a piece of cold toast as a snack.

berry baby bircher

Age: third month of eating, plus

Not suitable for freezing

Makes: 2 (some for bub, some for you)

Prep time: 1 minute

Cooking time: 3 minutes

¼ cup instant oats

½ cup apple juice

1 tablespoon full-fat plain or vanilla yoghurt

¼ cup berries of your choice (fresh or frozen is fine), chopped or pureed

A twist on a café favourite and another way to serve the goodness of oats.

Combine the oats, juice and ¼ cup of water in a microwave-safe jug and microwave on medium–high for 3 minutes, stirring once.

Stir the yoghurt and chopped or pureed berries through the cooked oats and serve.

> tip Here are some alternative fruit ideas: finely chopped pear, grated apple, stewed apricots or stewed rhubarb.

porridge, stewed apple and cinnamon

Age: second month of eating, plus

Not suitable for freezing

Makes: 2 (some for bub, some for you)

Prep time: 1 minute

Cooking time: 3 minutes

¼ cup instant oats

¾ cup full-fat milk

2 teaspoons (or 1 cube) apple puree

Pinch of ground cinnamon

A firm fave in our house. No matter what happens with the rest of the day, at least I know my kids have had a super-nourishing breakfast to get them started.

Combine the oats and milk in a saucepan and cook over low heat for 3–5 minutes, stirring frequently until thick. You may need to add a little extra milk (or water) depending on how low your stovetop goes. Alternatively, place the milk and oats in a microwave-safe jug and microwave on medium–high for 3 minutes, stirring once.

Stir in the apple and cinnamon and allow to cool a little before serving.

> tip I always have a container of stewed apple in the fridge and find that adding it cold to the hot porridge really speeds up the cooling process for hungry babies.

vita brit with pear puree and yoghurt

Age: second month of eating, plus

Not suitable for freezing

Makes: 1 serve

Prep time: 1 minute

Cooking time: 1 minute

1 Vita Brit biscuit

½ cup full-fat milk

2 teaspoons (or 1 cube) pear puree

2 teaspoons full-fat plain yoghurt

A quick and easy alternative to porridge. Vita Brits can be substituted with Weet-Bix or any other quality breakfast biscuit — just watch for sodium and sugar content.

Place the Vita Brit biscuit and milk in a microwave-safe jug and warm through for 30 seconds. Stir in the pear and yoghurt to combine well. The biscuit should be soft and the mixture only just warm. You may only want to start with half a biscuit, adjusting milk quantities as necessary, and work your way up from there.

Other fruit purees that work well include peach, apricot and strawberry.

> *tip* Have a batch of pear puree cubes in the freezer for use in breakfasts. Throw the frozen cube in with the milk and it should thaw in the same time.

yoghurt with fruit purees

Age: second month of eating, plus

Suitable for freezing

Makes: 1 serve

Prep time: 5 minutes

Cooking time: 10 minutes

1 tablespoon Jalna whole-milk plain yoghurt

1 cube fruit puree – apple, pear, mango or stone fruits (frozen strawberries or raspberries thawed and pureed also work well), thawed

This is perfect for breakfast or a second course any time of the day. There are many fruit yoghurts commercially available and some even claim to be specifically developed for babies. In my opinion these are still too sweet and are never as good as the real thing. Always use a full-fat plain yoghurt and rely on the sweetness of in-season fruit rather than added sugars to please your baby. They have a lifetime of sugary foods ahead of them so no need to rush into it. I like Jalna whole-milk plain yoghurt – the one with the blue lid.

Stir the fruit and yoghurt together and serve. Easy!

lunch

This is the time to introduce new flavours and textures. Remember, it can take up to 10 presentations of a particular food for your baby to decide to eat it. This can be frustrating, especially when you've cooked all this beautiful food that's not going to be eaten.

There were times I wanted to cry, but there's no point. Instead, I happily watched our dog put on much needed kilos. As I've said before, try not to despair. Always smile when you are feeding your baby and talk soothingly to them. I came up with a little ditty that was sung while feeding each meal and it really worked; in fact, we even had a dance mix when things really needed some spicing up! Remember to keep your eye out for the quick arm swipe that can send a bowl of food to the floor in the blink of an eye. This is probably the one thing that upset me more than anything. I'm not sure if it was the wastage or the cleaning that was hardest to deal with.

When first introducing meat, you need to do it slowly. Don't start with a bowl of meat casserole but rather with two cubes of casserole mixed with some veggie cubes, gradually altering the ratio. Try to prepare three or four different meals each week and rotate them to ensure your baby is getting a variety. In addition to the main meal, I always had some steamed or roasted veggie pieces in the fridge that I could warm and serve as finger food.

Herbs and gentle spice

Don't get stuck in the trap of thinking babies like bland food. They like what they know. Many of my recipes call for small amounts of spices to be added. These do not add heat in the chilli sense, but they do add a depth of flavour and help babies to differentiate between one mashed meal and another.

Preparation tips

• Use jars of crushed garlic to save time (1 teaspoon = 1 clove).

• Use salt-reduced stock powders, half strength, in the first months.

• When dicing veggies, think about the end product. If you're going to puree the dish, the dice size doesn't need to be too fine. If you are planning on only lightly mashing, then work to a smaller dice.

chicken, apple and pumpkin

Age: second month of eating, plus

Suitable for freezing

Makes: 2 cups

Prep time: 5 minutes

Cooking time: 25 minutes

2 teaspoons butter

½ onion (50 g), finely diced

2 chicken tenderloins, cut into 2 cm pieces

½ apple*, peeled, cored and diced

100 g (1 cup) diced butternut pumpkin

100 ml salt-reduced chicken stock

100 ml unsweetened apple juice

* Granny Smiths are the sourest of apples and although we generally use them in other cooking, you might want to opt for something a little sweeter in this dish.

This sweet and fruity chicken dish is a perfect way for your baby to try his or her first taste of meat. It's been a winning dish for many babies and the premise of fruit plus meat is a great trick for you to take forward in your repertoire. You'll be doubling this recipe in no time at all – use a full apple to one chicken breast, just to make it easier.

Melt the butter in a saucepan and sauté the onion for 5 minutes. Add all the other ingredients except the chicken and simmer for 20 minutes. Add the chicken and cook for a further 5–10 minutes until the pumpkin pieces are soft.

Puree to the desired consistency. Divide into portions and freeze.

tip Try gently roasting the pumpkin first to alter the flavour of this dish.

peachy chicken

Age: second month of eating, plus

Suitable for freezing

Makes: 1 cup

Prep time: 3 minutes

Cooking time: 15 minutes

1 chicken tenderloin, diced

2 canned peach halves, drained and roughly chopped

2 teaspoons white rice

150 ml salt-reduced chicken stock

Need I say more? Simple and delicious with the goodness of rice. Bon appétit!

Combine all the ingredients except the chicken in a saucepan and simmer for 10 minutes. Add the chicken and simmer for a further 5–10 minutes until the rice is cooked.

Puree to the desired consistency. If it's too thick, thin with either your baby's regular milk (breast or formula) or a dash of water.

apricot lamb

Age: second month of eating, plus

Suitable for freezing

Makes: 1½ cups

Prep time: 10 minutes

Cooking time: 1½ hours

1 tablespoon olive oil

1 onion, finely diced

1 carrot (100 g), peeled and finely diced

1 celery stick (60 g), stringy bits removed and finely diced

1 garlic clove, minced

2 lamb forequarter chops or 300 g diced lamb meat

1 cup salt-reduced vegetable stock

1 × 425 ml can apricot halves, drained and syrup reserved (you will need ½ cup syrup and 6 apricot halves)

150 g potato, peeled and finely diced

1 tablespoon chopped fresh parsley leaves

Remember the comfort of your Mum's apricot chicken, or lamb, oozing French Onion Soup packet mix? Now that's comfort food. This one's easy on the sodium-laced packet mix but you get the picture. I use chops in my casseroles as meat on the bone has more flavour and tends not to dry out as much, but feel free to used diced lamb from your butcher.

Preheat the oven to 160°C.

On the stovetop, heat the oil in a heavy-based casserole or ovenproof dish over medium heat and sauté the onion, carrot and celery for 5 minutes until translucent. Add the garlic and cook for 1 minute. Push the vegetables to the side of the pan, turn up the heat and brown the chops (or diced lamb) for 2 minutes on each side. Add the stock, apricot syrup and potatoes and stir well. Transfer to the oven and cook, covered, for 1 hour.

Finely chop the apricots and add to the casserole. Cook for a further 30 minutes, adding more water if necessary. Remove from the oven and carefully lift out the chops. Strip the meat from the bones and shred or dice finely.

Ensure all the potato chunks have broken down and mash slightly with a fork. Return the meat to the casserole and stir in the chopped parsley. Puree further as required. Divide into portions and freeze.

> tip Remaining apricot halves can be pureed and served with plain full-fat yoghurt.

red lentil dhal

Age: second month of eating, plus

Suitable for freezing

Makes: 2 cups

Prep time: 5 minutes

Cooking time: 30 minutes

½ butternut pumpkin, peeled and diced into 2 cm pieces*

2 tablespoons olive oil

2 teaspoons butter

½ small onion, finely diced

1 garlic clove, minced

¼ teaspoon ground coriander

¼ teaspoon ground cumin

½ cup red lentils

1½ cups salt-reduced chicken or veggie stock

Plain full-fat yoghurt

1 tablespoon chopped fresh coriander leaves

* You don't need all of this but leftovers can be used as finger food or in my Pumpkin and Sage Risotto (page 104) or Chicken Couscous (page 59).

I've always loved dhal. It's tasty, filling and good for you. This dish is so simple to make and super delicious. For older children, it's great served with warm roti bread, which is readily available from most supermarkets.

Preheat the oven to 180°C. Line an oven tray with baking paper.

Toss the pumpkin in 1 tablespoon of olive oil. Place on the baking tray and roast for 30 minutes, stirring occasionally. Check the pumpkin is soft all the way through before removing from the oven.

To make the dhal, heat a saucepan over medium heat. Add the remaining oil and the butter and sauté the onion for 5 minutes. Add the garlic and sauté for a further minute. Add the ground spices and stir until fragrant, about 30 seconds. Add the lentils and stock and simmer, covered, for 20 minutes, stirring occasionally, until soft and mushy. Add the chopped coriander.

Mash ¾ cup of roasted pumpkin pieces with a fork and stir into the cooked lentils until well combined.

Puree if required or leave as is. Serve warm with a dollop of yoghurt stirred through and some fresh coriander leaves as a garnish.

tip This dish will take you a long way – just adjust the spice levels as your baby grows.

quick chicken and mushroom risotto

Age: third month of eating, plus

Suitable for freezing

Makes: 1 serve

Prep time: 1 minute

Cooking time: 4 minutes

¼ cup rice flakes*

½ cup salt-reduced chicken stock

50 g chicken mince (or ½ chicken tenderloin, finely chopped)

3 button mushrooms, finely chopped

2 teaspoons parmesan or tasty cheese, grated

1–2 teaspoons ricotta cheese (optional)

Chopped fresh parsley leaves

* Available in the health food section of your supermarket or specialty health food stores.

This cheat's risotto is ready in 5 minutes flat. It's great for young babies getting used to new flavours and textures and a terrific speedy standby for toddlers. I love this dish as it's so easy to prepare and my kids love it!

Place all the ingredients except the cheeses in saucepan and simmer for 3–4 minutes, stirring regularly to break up the chicken mince. The rice flakes will soften and thicken to a porridge-like consistency.

Add the cheeses and stir to combine. Sprinkle with the chopped parsley for colour and freshness and allow to cool before serving.

For tasty variations on this dish, cook the rice flakes and stock as per above and:

- Replace the mushrooms with ¼ cup mashed pumpkin (steamed or roasted) to make a delicious pumpkin risotto

- Add ¼ cup roasted pumpkin and a cube of pear puree to the same quantity of rice flakes and cheeses to make a pumpkin and pear risotto

- Add ¼ cup cooked green peas and a few baby spinach leaves, washed and chopped, to make a green risotto

- Replace the chicken mince with finely chopped roast chicken (or any cooked chicken) and keep the cheeses for another tasty alternative.

tip Ricotta cheese is a great binding agent. Not only does it add a lovely mild flavour, it helps bind the risotto together on the spoon – a blessing for little people attempting to feed themselves.

braised lentils and pumpkin

Age: second month of eating, plus

Suitable for freezing

Makes: 1½ cups

Prep time: 10 minutes

Cooking time: 1 hour

1 tablespoon olive oil

1 small onion (100 g), diced

1 small carrot (100 g), peeled and diced

1 stick of celery, with stringy bits
removed, finely diced

1 garlic clove, crushed

½ cup brown or green lentils
(not the French-style Puy lentils which
hold their shape)

400 ml salt-reduced vegetable stock

75 g butternut pumpkin, peeled,
deseeded and finely diced

Lentils are a great protein alternative and expose babies to an interesting new texture. This dish differs from the Red Lentil Dhal (page 46) in colour, texture and flavour, as brown lentils are completely different from the red ones. You can also substitute some of the pumpkin for some peeled tomato pieces.

Heat the oil in a heavy-based saucepan over medium heat. Add the onion, carrot and celery and sauté for 5 minutes, stirring occasionally. Add the garlic and cook for 1 minute. Add the lentils and stock. Bring to the boil, lower the heat and simmer for 20 minutes. Add the pumpkin and simmer for a further 30 minutes until the lentils and pumpkin are very soft.

Puree to the desired consistency. Divide into portions.

This dish will naturally break down and become mushy with a longer cooking time, which you might like to try when first introducing texture.

tip For older babies, try adding a ¼ teaspoon of curry powder with the garlic to make this a curried lentil and pumpkin dish, garnishing with some chopped coriander.

mashed veggies

Age: second month of eating, plus

Not suitable for freezing

Makes: 1 cup

Prep time: 5 minutes

Cooking time: 10 minutes

1 small potato (100 g), peeled and roughly chopped

½ carrot (50 g), peeled and roughly chopped

½ cup (50 g) pumpkin or sweet potato pieces

50 g swede or zucchini, peeled and roughly chopped

½ cup frozen peas

½ teaspoon Vegemite

½ cup grated tasty cheese (optional)

An oldie but a goodie. The veggies listed here are more of a guide – just make sure whichever veggies you do use are fresh, full of flavour and well cooked.

Place the potato and carrot pieces in a saucepan and barely cover with water. Bring to the boil, lower the heat and simmer for 3 minutes. Add the pumpkin and swede pieces and cook for a further 5 minutes until all the veggies are tender, adding more water if necessary. Add the peas and cook for a further 2 minutes.

Strain off all but 1 tablespoon of cooking water, add the Vegemite and mash with a stick blender or a fork to your baby's preferred consistency.

These mashed veggies are delicious served with some grated tasty cheese stirred through.

Leftovers won't freeze well if you use potato but will keep for a few days in the fridge. If your baby doesn't seem to like potato (which many don't) simply omit it and freeze away.

> tip Cooking times will vary depending on the size of your diced veggies so check all veggies are tender before straining.

roasted salmon, pumpkin and sweet potato

Age: second month of eating, plus

Suitable for freezing

Makes: 2 cups

Prep time: 5 minutes

Cooking time: 30 minutes

100 g pumpkin, peeled and diced into 2 cm pieces

100 g sweet potato, peeled and diced into 2 cm pieces

1 tablespoon olive oil

150 g fillet of salmon, bones removed

¼ cup frozen peas

4 teaspoons grated tasty cheese

Roasted pumpkin and sweet potato lend a lovely natural sweetness to this goodness-packed first taste of fish. Just make sure there are no bones in your salmon before you cook it.

Preheat the oven to 180°C. Line a small tray with baking paper.

Place the pumpkin and sweet potato pieces on the lined tray and drizzle with the olive oil. Roast for 20 minutes. Add the salmon fillet and roast for a further 7–10 minutes. If your veggies are getting too much colour remove them from the oven, as you don't want too much of a crust on them.

Meanwhile, steam the peas in the microwave according to packet directions.

Remove the veggies from the oven and mash the pumpkin and sweet potato with the tasty cheese (you may need to microwave the mix quickly to help melt the cheese). Remove the skin from the salmon and flake with a fork, double-checking for any bones as you go.

Combine the mash, peas and salmon. Puree to the desired consistency or leave as is. Divide into portions and freeze.

> tip Add a cube of cheese sauce to this dish to alter its flavour and texture.

greek lamb casserole

Age: second month of eating, plus

Suitable for freezing

Makes: 2½ cups

Prep time: 15 minutes

Cooking time: 1½ hours

1 tablespoon olive oil

1 onion (100 g), diced

1 carrot (100 g), diced

300 g lamb, diced into small, even pieces
(or 460 g forequarter chops)

1 garlic clove, crushed

1 small eggplant (200 g), diced

1 small zucchini (100 g), diced

500 ml salt-reduced chicken stock

100 ml passata* or 2 tomatoes, diced

½ teaspoon dried oregano or 3–4 sprigs
of fresh oregano

½–1 teaspoon ground cinnamon
(depending on your baby's developing tastes)

⅓ cup risoni pasta

* Passata is available in supermarkets but can be
substituted with canned diced tomatoes.

Inspired by moussaka, this dish is mildly flavoured with a delicate sweetness from the cinnamon and a silkiness from the veggies. The risoni provides a carbohydrate so it's a complete meal that freezes well.

Heat the olive oil in a casserole dish over medium heat. Add the onion and carrot and sauté for 5 minutes. Add the lamb and brown off for 3 minutes. Add the garlic and cook for 1 minute. Add the diced veggies, stock and passata (or diced tomatoes) and bring to a simmer. Add the oregano and cinnamon, reduce the heat to very low and simmer, covered, for 1½ hours. The lamb should be tender enough for you to break it up with your spoon. If the meat is not breaking up easily, continue to simmer for a further 15 minutes or until the meat falls apart.

Add the risoni and stir well. Continue cooking for 15 minutes, stirring occasionally, until the risoni is soft and the casserole is thick. Any excess liquid will be absorbed while the dish cools.

Depending on the age of your baby, you may wish to puree all or half of the casserole to create a texture to his or her taste

Divide into portions and freeze.

tip Like any slow-cooked dish, this one only gets better with time, so allow it to sit in the fridge in an airtight container for a day before freezing portions.

aussie beef casserole

Age: second month of eating, plus

Suitable for freezing

Makes: 2 cups, including sweet potato

Prep time: 15 minutes

Cooking time: 1½ hours

1 tablespoon olive oil

1 small onion (100 g), finely diced

1 small carrot (100 g), peeled and diced

1 small stick of celery with strings removed, diced

½ garlic clove, minced

2 teaspoons plain flour

200 g casserole beef (try to use chuck or gravy beef, removing excess fat), diced

1 teaspoon Vegemite

150 g (1 cup) diced sweet potato

This is a simple first casserole to start your baby on beef. By adding the side veggies to the actual casserole, you can have a complete meal in a cube and then play with other flavour additions such as Cheesy Sauce (page 80). This may take a while to cook but it's important to make sure the meat is as tender as possible or your baby will struggle to chew it. And remember, it's cooking time not preparation time.

Heat the oil in a casserole dish over medium heat and sauté the onion, carrot and celery for 5 minutes, stirring occasionally. Add the garlic and sauté for a further 1 minute.

Place the flour in a separate bowl, add the beef and lightly toss to coat. Push the veggies to one side of the casserole dish, add the beef and lightly brown. Add the Vegemite and 1 cup of water and simmer, covered, over low heat for 1½ hours until the beef is super tender. Alternatively, cook in a 160°C oven for 1½ hours.

Puree to the desired consistency. Divide into portions and freeze.

Serve with mashed sweet potato and a sprinkle of fresh parsley. Alternatively, you could add cubes of sweet potato to the casserole for the last 30 minutes of cooking.

> tip For a different spin, serve with mashed carrot and swede. Simply steam or boil a carrot and a small swede until tender and then mash as you would a potato.

chicken couscous

Age: second month of eating, plus

Suitable for freezing

Makes: 1½ cups

Prep time: 3 minutes

Cooking time: 5 minutes

1 tablespoon olive oil

1 spring onion, white part only
(or a few chives), finely chopped

½ teaspoon ground cinnamon

½ teaspoon ground coriander

100 g chicken mince (or a small handful of
leftover cooked chicken), finely chopped

½ small zucchini (50 g), grated

¼ cup roasted pumpkin pieces (or grate
a small piece of fresh pumpkin to give you
about ¼ cup; it will cook with the chicken)

1 cup salt-reduced chicken stock

⅓ cup couscous

Chopped fresh coriander leaves (optional)

This dish is super quick to prepare, has great flavour and
can be pureed down. Better still, the nature of the finished
product is great for introducing a little texture.

Heat the oil in a small saucepan.

Add the spring onions (or chives) and stir for 30 seconds.

Add the spices and stir for another 30 seconds.

Add all the remaining ingredients and cook, covered, for
3 minutes, stirring occasionally to avoid sticking.

Serve with a sprinkling of chopped fresh coriander if you
have some.

tip The flavour in this dish can be altered and enhanced with a smidge
of garlic and some sultanas or raisins thrown in during cooking.

bolognaise for little people

Age: third month of eating, plus

Suitable for freezing

Makes: 2½ cups (it is a lot but it's so good it seems a shame to cook any less and it freezes beautifully)

Prep time: 15 minutes

Cooking time: 1½ hours

1 tablespoon olive oil

1 onion (100 g), peeled and finely diced

1 small carrot (100 g), peeled and finely diced

1 stick of celery with stringy bits removed, finely diced

½ garlic clove, minced

100 g beef mince

100 g pork mince

1 cup full-fat milk

¼ teaspoon ground nutmeg

2 teaspoons tomato paste

1 cup salt-reduced beef stock

A few fresh basil leaves or a shake of dried basil

5 button mushrooms (100 g), finely chopped

Pasta, to serve

Grated parmesan cheese, to serve

No freezer should ever be without some bolognaise. I don't know about your traditional recipe, but my bolognaise is usually loaded with wine and other rich flavours. Somehow I just didn't feel right giving my kids a bolognaise that had half a bottle of red in it, so I came up with this variation. While you might think it odd, the milk helps to tenderise the meat and soften its flavour, resulting in a more delicate and creamy bolognaise. Plus it has the advantage of contributing to the daily dairy requirement.

If your baby's bottom is sensitive to tomato-based foods, this sauce might just work for you, as the milk also cuts the acidity. Try it. You might end up putting milk in your own regular bolognaise, like I now do.

Heat a medium-sized heavy-based saucepan, with a lid. Add the olive oil and sauté the onion, carrot and celery for about 5 minutes over medium heat. Add the garlic and cook for 1 minute. Turn up the heat and add the minced meats. Brown for about 3–5 minutes, stirring well. Add the milk and nutmeg and simmer for 5 minutes. Add the tomato paste and stir to combine. Add the beef stock and simmer, covered, for 20 minutes. Add the basil and mushrooms and simmer for a further 20 minutes.

Serve with your baby's favourite pasta and some parmesan.

The beauty of bolognaise is that it can grow with your baby. Start by pureeing the finished sauce with the cooked pasta and then progress to tiny soup or baby pasta shapes and then to larger pasta shapes, changing the texture of the sauce as you go by altering the size and combination of the diced veggies.

Leftover sauce should be divided into portions and frozen. Need more greens? Try adding peas or finely chopped broccoli pieces along with the mushrooms.

tuna pasta

Age: second month of eating, plus

Suitable for freezing

Makes 1½ cups

Prep time: 3 minutes

Cooking time: 10 minutes

½ cup dried soup pasta or other small pasta shape

1 tablespoon olive oil

1 onion (100 g), finely diced

½ garlic clove, minced

1 × 95 g can of tuna in springwater (this is milder than tuna in brine or oil)

1 tablespoon tomato paste

100 ml cream (or ⅓ cup Cheesy Sauce – see page 80)

Chopped fresh parsley leaves

Grated parmesan or tasty cheese

Canned tuna will become one of your best friends in the kitchen, so try to get your baby used to it from early on. Not only is it affordable, readily available and happy sitting quietly in the pantry, it's delicious and good for us!

Cook the pasta according to packet directions, omitting salt.

Meanwhile, heat the olive oil in a frying pan over medium–low heat. Add the onion and sauté for 5 minutes, stirring occasionally. Add the garlic and cook for a further minute.

Add the drained tuna, using a fork to break it up. Add the tomato paste and stir well to combine. Cook for a further 2 minutes. Add the cream, stir and heat through – do not boil. Remove from the heat and stir in the parsley.

When the sauce is ready, stir through the cooked, drained pasta and puree to the desired consistency. When serving, don't forget to add a sprinkling of cheese

Divide the remaining quantity into portions and freeze.

 tip This sauce works equally well with boiled rice. I have found some babies are fussier with boiled rice than with pasta, but see how you go. Also, try adding a veggie base cube to the meal as you are re-heating it. This works brilliantly with broccoli, cauliflower, spinach or pea purees.

carrot and zucchini pasta

Age: third month of eating, plus

Suitable for freezing

Makes: 1½ cups

Prep time: 5 minutes

Cooking time: 15 minutes

½ tablespoon olive oil

1 tablespoon butter

1 carrot (100 g), peeled and grated

1 zucchini (100 g), grated

2 brussels sprouts with
outer leaves and core removed,
finely sliced (optional)

¾ cup dried soup pasta or other
small pasta shape

½ cup shaved tasty cheese

This recipe helps introduce subtle texture to meals but can also be blended for younger or texture-fussy babies. This combination is very effective at masking other veggies, so you can ensure a goodness-packed meal. Brussels sprouts or broccoli work well.

Heat a frying pan over medium heat, add the olive oil and butter and heat until bubbling. Add the grated veggies and the brussels sprouts (if using) and stir well. Cook for about 10 minutes, stirring occasionally, until all the veggies are soft.

Meanwhile, cook the pasta according to packet directions. Spoon 2 tablespoons of cooking water into the veggies and drain the pasta. Add the pasta to the veggie mix with the tasty cheese and stir to combine.

Puree to the desired consistency or leave as is and serve.

Divide into portions and freeze until required.

dinner [soups]

Witching hour is a crazy phenomenon among babies. You can ease the distress of both yourself and your baby by serving a simple and nutritious dinner that your baby can easily eat and digest.

A simple dinner is a fitting end to a big day. We found soups to be the ultimate dinner. They are easy to make, easy to freeze, offer great nutritional value and are terrific for tired babies. Simple pastas and other comfort foods are also ideal.

The following are a few of our favourite soups but no doubt you've got your own recipes that, with a little modifying, will be perfect for your little bub. Just be sure to reduce the liquid quantity to ensure they are thick enough to stay put on the spoon.

Serve thick soups with buttered toast soldiers or mini cream cheese sandwich triangles and encourage your littlies to dip them into the soup. And, of course, any of my lunch recipes are suitable as dinner options as well.

leek and potato soup

Age: second month of eating, plus

Suitable for freezing

Makes: 3 cups

Prep time: 10 minutes

Cooking time: 20 minutes

1 large leek (400 g)

1 tablespoon olive oil

1 tablespoon butter

1 small onion (100 g), sliced

1 garlic clove, sliced

2 potatoes (250–300 g), peeled and chopped into chunks

1 small zucchini (100 g), chopped into 2.5 cm rounds

1½ cups salt-reduced vegetable or chicken stock

100 ml cream

Chopped fresh parsley leaves

This soup was such a hit in our house that it almost got embarrassing. It seemed that whenever I served it, a particular friend of mine was either at our house or on the phone. I had to assure her that I did actually serve other meals, sometimes! Great big helpings will always get eaten, giving you the best hope of a solid night's sleep.

Forgive me if you already know this but leeks are terrific harbourers of dirt and there is nothing worse than preparing a meal only to discover it is ruined by grit. So, to prepare leeks, trim off most of the green part and discard. Remove and discard the tip at the root end. Slice the leek in half lengthways. Now slice each leek half into thin half-moons (about 5 mm). Place your sliced leek in a large bowl of water and wash thoroughly. If you have a salad spinner, spin to dry well, otherwise just tip the leek slices into a colander and let them drain while you prepare everything else.

For the soup, heat the oil and butter in a saucepan over medium heat. Add the onion and leek and cook, stirring for 5–7 minutes until translucent and soft, but not browned. Add the garlic and sauté for 1 minute. Add the potatoes and zucchini, stirring to coat. Add the stock and bring to the boil, then lower the heat and simmer for 10–15 minutes until the potatoes are soft. Remove from the heat.

Blend with a stick blender until smooth, adding a little more water if it is too thick. Add the cream and parsley. Stir well.

Divide into portions and freeze.

broccoli soup

Age: third month of eating, plus

Suitable for freezing

Makes: 2 cups

Prep time: 10 minutes

Cooking time: 15 minutes

1 tablespoon olive oil

1 onion (100 g), roughly chopped

1 garlic clove, roughly chopped (add more
as your baby gets older)

50 g bacon (about 1 rasher)

1 small head of broccoli (300 g), roughly
chopped, including some of the stalk

1 small zucchini (150 g), roughly chopped

1 potato (150 g), peeled and
roughly chopped

400 ml salt-reduced chicken stock

100 ml cream or full-fat milk

Buttered toast triangles or cream cheese
sandwiches, to serve

My friend's mum makes the best broccoli soup. I remember
it as a kid and I still get soup-envy when she gets a batch
delivered by her mum. It's one of those things that, if you
get it right and disguise just how good for you it really
is, then you're on a winner. You'll be cooking this, or a
souped-up (pardon the pun) version, for years to come.

Heat a medium-sized saucepan on the stove and add the oil
and onion. Sauté for 5 minutes. Add the garlic, bacon and all the
veggies. Stir over the heat for 5 minutes and then add the stock.
Bring to boil then reduce the heat, cover and simmer for
10–15 minutes until all the veggies are soft.

Remove from the heat and blend with a stick blender until
smooth, being careful not to splash yourself. Slowly add the
cream or milk, ensuring the soup does not become too runny.
(This soup is designed to be on the thicker side to help it hold
on the spoon.)

Serve with buttered toast triangles or cream cheese sandwiches.

Freeze the remaining soup in individual portions.

cheesymite soup

Age: second month of eating, plus

Suitable for freezing

Makes: 2½ cups

Prep time: 3 minutes

Cooking time: 15 minutes

400 g cauliflower (about half a head), roughly chopped

500 ml salt-reduced chicken stock

½ teaspoon Vegemite

60 ml full-fat milk

½ cup grated tasty cheese

2 teaspoons parmesan cheese

Chopped fresh parsley leaves

Buttery Vegemite toast soldiers, to serve

In truth, it's a cauliflower soup but Cheesymite just makes it sound so much yummier – which is important, as it is delicious and it shouldn't be let down by a name. Oh, and it's so very, very simple.

Combine the cauliflower and stock in a saucepan and cook for 15 minutes until soft. Add the Vegemite and stir.

Remove from the heat and blend with a stick blender, being careful not to splash yourself. The soup is likely to be a bit thick at this stage, so gradually add the milk and continue to blend until you have a smooth consistency. Try to keep it reasonably thick to ensure it holds on the spoon. Stir in the cheeses.

Serve with a little fresh parsley sprinkled on top to give it some zing. Buttery Vegemite toast soldiers make a great accompaniment.

 tip Don't use too much tasty cheese as the soup will become stringy. If you don't have parmesan on hand simply omit – it will still be delicious.

corn chowder

Age: second month of eating, plus

Suitable for freezing

Makes: 2 cups

Prep time: 5 minutes

Cooking time: 25 minutes

¼ onion (about 30 g), peeled and roughly chopped

1 potato (about 130 g), peeled and roughly chopped

1 small carrot (about 100 g), peeled and roughly chopped

1 bay leaf, fresh or dried

300 ml full-fat milk

1 fresh corn cob, peeled and kernels removed (or 1 cup frozen kernels)

Fresh bread or toast, to serve

The natural sweetness of corn makes this soup really appealing and the use of milk is a great way to beef up your bub's dairy intake.

Place the onion, potato, carrot and bay leaf in a saucepan. Cover with milk and bring to the boil over medium heat. Reduce the heat and simmer for 10 minutes. Add the corn kernels and simmer for a further 15 minutes until all the veggies are soft.

Remove from the heat and discard the bay leaf.

Puree the chowder until smooth using a stick blender, adding more milk if necessary. Corn is notoriously hard to puree – you may like to pass it through a sieve to remove any husks, but I never did. It's all good roughage!

Serve with fresh bread or toast for dipping.

tip For older children, add crispy bacon bits and serve with some grated cheese on top.

minestrone soup

Age: second month of eating, plus

Suitable for freezing

Makes: 4 cups

Prep time: 10 minutes

Cooking time: 35 minutes

1 tablespoon olive oil

1 small onion (100 g), roughly chopped

1 carrot (100 g), peeled and finely diced

1 celery stick (100 g) with stringy bits removed, finely diced

1 garlic clove, minced

1 bay leaf, fresh or dried

1 cup passata or canned diced tomatoes

1½ cups salt-reduced beef or chicken stock

¼ cup dried soup pasta (any very small pasta shape will do, incuding broken spaghetti pieces, macaroni or shells)

1 potato (130 g), peeled and finely diced

50 g white cabbage, finely shredded or diced

7 green beans (50 g), trimmed and cut into small rounds

1 × 125 g can of four-bean mix

Chopped fresh parsley leaves

Buttered toast soldiers, to serve

Traditionally, minestrone is more of a broth with vegetables, beans and pasta. In this version, however, you can blend as much or as little of the soup as you like, altering the texture to best suit your baby's eating capabilities. When dicing your veggies think about the end texture. If you plan on leaving it pretty chunky, do a fine dice that your baby can manage.

Heat the oil in a saucepan large enough to hold the soup.

Add the onion, carrot, celery, garlic and bay leaf and sauté for 5 minutes.

Add the passata and stock and simmer for 15 minutes.

Add the pasta, potato, cabbage and beans (green and tinned) and simmer for 15 minutes until all the veggies are soft.

Remove from the heat and discard the bay leaf. Puree part or all of the soup to the desired consistency.

Serve the soup sprinkled with parmesan and chopped fresh parsley, with buttered toast soldiers on the side.

Freeze the remaining soup in individual portions.

pumpkin soup

Age: second month of eating, plus

Suitable for freezing

Makes: 3 cups

Prep time: 5 minutes

Cooking time: 20 minutes

1 tablespoon olive oil

1 tablespoon butter

1 small onion (100 g), sliced

¼ butternut pumpkin (400 g), peeled and diced

1 garlic clove, roughly chopped

½ green apple (100 g), peeled, cored and chopped

1 cup salt-reduced vegetable or chicken stock

1 teaspoon brown sugar (optional)

Pinch of ground cinnamon or nutmeg

Water or milk, to thin

Chopped fresh parsley leaves

Cream cheese sandwiches, to serve

Who doesn't love a good pumpkin soup? Need I say more?

Heat the oil and butter in a saucepan over medium–low heat. Add the onion and stir for 5 minutes until translucent and soft, but not browned.

Add the pumpkin and garlic and sauté for 1 minute. Add the apple and stock and bring to the boil, then lower the heat and simmer for 10–15 minutes until the pumpkin is soft.

Remove from the heat and add the sugar (if using) and spice.

Blend with a stick blender until smooth, adding water or milk as necessary. The soup should be thick enough to hold well on your baby's spoon.

Sprinkle over the parsley and serve with cream cheese sandwiches.

Freeze the remaining soup in individual portions.

finger food

When your baby's pincer grip starts to develop and he or she can pick up small objects (around 8 or 9 months), it's time to try finger food. Eating finger food is important developmentally, but remember that every baby is different in their likes and dislikes, and some will not take to finger food as well as others. It's not so much that they can't do it, but some simply seem to prefer using a spoon. Don't be alarmed if your baby shows a preference for one style of meal over another. Simply cater for their needs, but ensure you mix it up a bit and offer lots of variety. Try using finger foods as snacks if your baby prefers to eat meals with a spoon.

Ideal finger foods at this stage are tender cooked carrot, sweet potato and pumpkin pieces; cooked pasta shapes; bread and rusks; chopped melon or other soft fruits; fish or meat patties broken up; cubes of ripe avocado and ripe bananas.

Remember, your baby must always be supervised when eating because of the risk of choking.

homemade rusks

Age: third month of eating, plus

Not suitable for freezing

Makes: 16 rusks

Prep time: 5 minutes

Cooking time: 20 minutes

4 bread slices, preferably wholemeal, crusts removed

1 teaspoon Vegemite

½ cup finely grated tasty cheese (optional)

Making your own rusks is not only a great way to use up old bread, it's a whole lot cheaper than buying the commercial ones. Although these are quite different in texture, they are loved by babies and help to introduce them to different flavours. And you are less likely to find half-eaten, soggy ones discarded all around your living room, car or pram.

Preheat the oven to 120°C. Line an oven tray with baking paper.

Dissolve the Vegemite in 100 ml of boiling water. Lay the bread slices on the baking tray and liberally brush both sides with the Vegemite-infused water. You want to cover them well but not such much that they fall apart. Quickly cut each slice of bread into four lengths (soldiers).

Place the tray in the middle of the oven. After 10 minutes, brush the bread with the Vegemite water again. Cook for a further 10 minutes – they should be hardening up but not burning. Brush with more Vegemite water and sprinkle with cheese, if using. Continue cooking for another 10 minutes. Remove and cool on a wire rack. Store in an airtight container.

For a variation on this recipe, try using Bonox instead of Vegemite. Bonox is a terrific beef-flavoured product that will add variety to your baby's diet while also getting them used to beefy flavours.

tip Use the thicker 'toast cut' bread slices as they will be more rewarding for your baby's gums.

max out on veggies

I have always found it handy to have prepared veggie bases in the freezer. These allow me to add hits of nutritious veggies to any meal, or to quickly whip up a meal when I'm caught short.

Veggie bases can be plain (any of your first purees) or blends such as Cheesy Veg (page 80). The satisfaction I get from watching my babies devour a bolognaise that has a cube or two of pureed broccoli stirred through it is immense.

We all know the basic rule of 'fresh is best' and want our children to be adaptable eaters, so seeing them eat lots of veggies that you know are fresh, unadulterated and cooked well will fill you with a real sense of pride and achievement.

And don't forget the joy of frozen peas. They are a wonderful resource, snap frozen to retain all their goodness.

waste not, want not

All too often we strain our veggies and discard the cooking water. Unfortunately, this is where much of the goodness now resides. Use the cooking water to help thin veggies when mashing or pureeing them. Even better, allow the flavoured water to cool and offer it to your baby as a tasty drink. They'll love it.

spinach puree

Age: second month of eating, plus

Suitable for freezing

Makes: ⅓ cup

Prep time: 5 minutes

Cooking time: 2 minutes

150 g baby spinach leaves, washed and stalks removed

Popeye taught us that eating spinach helps us grow big and strong so don't be afraid to get your baby eating spinach from a very early age. It's great added to just about anything from pastas to casseroles and a frozen cube thrown in here and there can really help to make you feel quite virtuous as a parent.

Heat a large frying pan over medium heat and add the spinach leaves (the water on the leaves from the washing process should be enough moisture for the cooking process). Spinach cooks quickly and shrinks down in no time at all so, using tongs, keep the leaves moving in the pan, tossing and turning until they are all wilted (about 2 minutes). Remove from the heat and allow to cool. Spinach holds a lot of moisture so you shouldn't need to add any additional liquid for pureeing.

Puree to the desired consistency and freeze in ice cube trays.

tip Try using frozen spinach instead. Simply snap off a convenient cube and use it in cooking.

roasted pumpkin

Age: second month of eating, plus

Suitable for freezing

Makes: 20 pieces

Prep time: 5 minutes

Cooking time: 10 minutes

1 tablespoon olive oil

½ butternut pumpkin (150 g), peeled, deseeded and cut into 2 cm pieces

Tiny sprinkling of thyme leaves (optional)

A simple pumpkin puree is raised to a whole new level by roasting the pumpkin first. Mashed roasted pumpkin can be added to lots of meals, or whole pieces can be served as a delicious finger food. Why not double the recipe and toss the roasted pumpkin through cooked pasta with some feta cheese and baby spinach leaves for your own dinner?

Preheat the oven to 180°C.

Toss the pumpkin in the olive oil and thyme (if using) and spread over a baking tray. Roast for 30 minutes, turning occasionally, until tender and starting to caramelise.

Remove from the oven and allow to cool slightly. Mash using a stick blender or leave whole. The mash can be frozen in portions.

> tip Store whole roasted pieces in the fridge and microwave to warm through before serving as finger food.

grated carrot and zucchini

Age: second month of eating, plus

Suitable for freezing

Makes: 2 cups

Prep time: 5 minutes

Cooking time: 10 minutes

½ tablespoon olive oil

1 tablespoon butter

1 carrot (100 g), peeled and grated

1 zucchini (100 g), grated

I use this combo all the time. I've nearly always got the ingredients on hand, it's super easy and the sweet flavour of the slowly sautéed veggies is loved by one and all. This is essentially the vegetable base of Carrot and Zucchini Pasta (page 64), but it's great as a frozen back-up to add to lots of different things.

Heat the olive oil and butter in a frying pan over medium heat until bubbling. Add the grated veggies and stir well.

Cook for about 10 minutes, stirring occasionally, until the veggies are soft.

Divide into portions and freeze.

cheesy veg

Age: second month of eating, plus

Suitable for freezing

Makes: 2 cups

Prep time: 5 minutes

Cooking time: 10 minutes

Cheese sauce (makes 1 cup)

2 teaspoons butter

10 g (about 2 teaspoons) plain flour

125 ml full-fat milk

¼ cup grated tasty cheese

Pinch of nutmeg (optional)

Steamed vegetables (makes 1 cup)

125 g (1 cup) chopped broccoli

125 g (1 cup) chopped cauliflower

1 carrot, peeled and chopped

This dish is as good as it sounds. It can be used for very young babies still experiencing first tastes or added to other dishes such as bolognaise or beef casserole to increase the veggie content. My microwave cheese sauce makes it easy-as and is guaranteed to be lump free.

Cheese sauce Place the butter in a jug and microwave for 20 seconds to melt. Add the flour, give it a quick stir and return to the microwave for 30 seconds to cook off the flour. Add the milk and whisk well. Microwave for 90 seconds, remove and whisk again. Cook for a further 30 seconds, remove and add the cheese and a small sprinkling of nutmeg (optional). Stir.

Steamed vegetables Steam or microwave the veggies until tender under a fork. The carrot will take the longest so give it a few minutes head start. Use a stick blender to chop or roughly puree the veggies.

Add to the cheese sauce and stir through. Allow to cool before dividing into cubes and freezing for future use.

cheesy sauce

Age: second month of eating, plus

Suitable for freezing

Makes: 3 cups (a large quantity ideal for lasagne or frozen cubes)

Prep time: 1 minute

Cooking time: 7 minutes for stovetop, 3 minutes for microwave

1 tablespoon butter

1 tablespoon plain flour

500 ml (2 cups) full-fat milk

½ cup grated tasty cheese

Pinch of nutmeg (optional)

Not only is cheese sauce a favourite comfort food, it is a terrific cube to have on hand to throw into meals to bulk up dairy intake. It can be made on the stovetop or just as easily in the microwave – the choice is yours.

Stovetop Melt the butter in a saucepan over medium heat, add the flour and cook for 1–2 minutes, stirring constantly to make a roux. Heat the milk in a separate saucepan for about 1 minute. Remove from the heat and add the milk to the roux a little at a time, stirring well to avoid lumps. Continue until all the milk is added. Return to a low heat and stir until thick. Remove from the heat and add the cheese and a sprinkle of nutmeg (if using). Stir.

Microwave Place the butter in a 1-litre microwave-safe jug and microwave for 20 seconds. Add the flour, stir and return to the microwave for 30 seconds to cook off the flour. Add the milk and whisk well. Microwave for 90 seconds, remove and whisk again. Cook for a further 30 seconds, remove and add the cheese and a sprinkle of nutmeg (optional). Stir.

helpful things to know

Here's an odd assortment of facts and tidbits I found useful along the way, or discovered and shared, much to the amazement and appreciation of my parents' group, friends and other young parents.

1. Sausage skins, especially frankfurts, can be chewy and cause choking, so peel them off before giving the meat to babies.

2. Corn husks. The little husk surrounding a corn kernel can be tricky for babies to swallow so if you have a Mouli use this to puree your corn. Otherwise blend corn dishes for a longer period and pass through a sieve to remove larger husks.

3. Despite chicken often being considered a bland meat, in my experience many babies do not like it on its own. If you are not pureeing the meal, opt for chicken mince in your cooking, where the texture is completely different.

4. Beef is another flavour that isn't always a hit. Make sure your dishes are well flavoured with other ingredients or try using a small amount of Bonox with mashed veggies to help babies adjust to the taste of beef.

5. Meat can be quite chewy. Tenderise it with a good bashing before cooking. If your baby still doesn't like pieces of cooked meat, stick with recipes using mince.

6. Cheesy Sauce (page 80) is a godsend. Have cubes in the freezer to add to meals, especially if your baby starts to cut down on his or her usual milk intake. It's a rich and tasty way of contributing to milk targets.

7. Mashed potato is commonly rejected by babies. I can hardly believe it, but it's true! Luckily there are many other great veggies that can be substituted.

8. Opposing teeth. Apparently my babies were well behind on dealing with chopped food according to all the literature and graphs (don't you love it when you fall outside the 'average'?). I found that they weren't really up for chewing larger textured meals until they had opposing front teeth and could really give it a good workout. So I recommend going at your own pace and knowing that it will eventually all fall into place.

9. When they don't eat – oh goodness! This can be stressful, distressing, annoying, heartbreaking and confidence smashing. Can I come up with any more appropriate feelings? The best advice I can give is to just relax (as best you can), try not to make a big deal of it and move on to the next thing. Babies typically won't starve themselves. If they are hungry they will eat. If you do have concerns about your baby's weight then see your health professional.

10. Boiled rice is another food I would have thought babies would love, but not necessarily. I know lots of babies who didn't come round to cooked rice until they were 18 months, plus. If your baby seems to resist rice then try using rice flakes as an alternative.

eggs

Eggs are a super-handy food. They are good for you, packed with protein, easy to prepare and keep well. But, they are also a common cause of allergies. If your baby can eat them, you have an instant repertoire of quick and easy meals but if not, you need to know.

My maternal health nurse once gave me an invaluable piece of advice: once people see your baby eating solids they make assumptions and it is inevitable that someone, someday soon, will offer them a cake or muffin or something containing eggs. It's best to be one step in front and try your baby on eggs. In my case, it happened just two days after my nurse told me this. It was my sister-in-law's fortieth birthday lunch and I looked up to find Sophie happily devouring her first ever piece of cake. She was seven months old.

I tested her the very next morning and discovered a slight intolerance – a minor redness around the mouth and chin. After a pacifying call to the Maternal and Child Health hotline, I simply waited another month before trying eggs again and we have never looked back. But the moral of the story is, try your baby on eggs in a safe and controlled environment before someone else does it for you. A tiny taste of your egg one morning is enough for you to know.

scrambled eggs

Age: third month of eating, plus (if egg-friendly)

Not suitable for freezing

Makes: 1 serving

Prep time: 1 minute

Cooking time: 4 minutes

1–2 free-range eggs, depending on appetite

2 teaspoons full-fat milk

1 dash Tabasco sauce (optional, but my kids always loved it)

2 teaspoons butter

2 teaspoons grated tasty cheese (optional)

Chopped fresh parsley leaves

Make sure you have tested your baby for egg intolerance first. Once you are in the clear, scrambled eggs are likely to become a super stand-in for any occasion. Acceptable as breakfast, lunch or dinner, they are packed with goodness and can be jazzed up to suit your baby's tastes.

Whisk the egg, milk and Tabasco (if using) together in a bowl.

Heat the butter in a small non-stick frying pan over medium heat. When bubbling, add the egg mix. Turn the heat to low and stir with a wooden spoon until curds form (about 1–2 minutes). Remove from the heat just before the eggs are fully set, as they will continue to cook. Add the cheese (if using) and stir well.

Serve the eggs sprinkled with chopped parsley and watch them disappear.

> *tip* Scrambled eggs are also great with some shredded ham or chopped tomato stirred through.

no looking back

no looking back

So your baby has been on solids for a good few months now. Your baby's repertoire of foods has grown and he or she is no doubt displaying definite likes and dislikes.

And it's probably around this stage that you are starting to get a bit stuck in a rut. Of course it's a big job cooking your regular family meal and providing a nutritious balanced diet for bub. These recipes will hopefully keep you inspired over the coming months and leave you with some fail-safe favourites to carry into the future. And don't forget favourites from the past few months – any of those meals left unpureed are great for older babies too.

Breakfast

You can expand your repertoire of brekkie options as your baby starts to deal with texture, but it will still be limited. Continue to keep away from sugar-loaded commercial cereals and stick with the basics such as porridge with apple puree.

Lunch and dinner

You can be a bit more flexible by this stage, but bear in mind both babies and toddlers are crankier in the evenings. Even when my bubs were 18 months old, I was still providing their main meal (protein) at lunchtime. It worked for us, but do what works for you.

independent feeding

You will go from runny purees to thick mashes and eventually to finely chopped food. In my experience, there is a balancing act between the right texture (chopped and small pieces) and the 'eatability' of the meal. Toddlers can become very independent beings and insist on feeding themselves.

This is great when it's working, as you get to do some tidying in the kitchen. But if the meal is too 'piecey', you will find it falling off the wobbly spoon before it makes it to your toddler's mouth, resulting in frustration, tears and tantrums.

To counter this I discovered the wonder of ricotta cheese.

It's relatively bland in flavour, goes with lots of things and works terrifically as a binding agent. A spoon of ricotta stirred into just about anything from a pasta bolognaise to a casserole helps hold the pieces together, resulting in a more satisfying meal for your baby. Just make sure that the base of the meal is well flavoured so that everything doesn't taste like a bowl of ricotta.

pantry staples

Aside from a freezer full of pre-cooked meals, having a few staples on hand can help make mealtimes much easier and calmer. My faves are:

- Rice flakes
- Couscous
- Baby pasta (small pasta shapes)
- Minced chicken and lamb frozen in 50 g portions
- Full-fat plain yoghurt
- Fruit puree cubes
- Free-range eggs
- Carrots
- Zucchini
- Frozen peas
- Onions
- Jars of passata (Italian tomato sauce) or tins of diced tomatoes
- Ricotta cheese and tasty cheese
- Full-fat milk
- Canned tuna
- Fresh parsley, preferably from your own garden
- A simple range of spices

chicken curry

Age: fourth month of eating, plus

Suitable for freezing

Makes: 4 cups
(I know this is lots but it freezes beautifully and the whole family will love it!)

Prep time: 5 minutes

Cooking time: 25 minutes

1 Granny Smith apple, peeled and cored

1 tablespoon vegetable or cooking oil

1 small onion (100 g), finely diced

1 garlic clove, minced

½ teaspoon mild curry powder

¼ small butternut pumpkin (200 g), peeled and diced

250 ml (1 cup) salt-reduced chicken stock

1 cup coconut milk

1 small head of broccoli (about 100 g), stalk included but chopped separately

1 chicken thigh (about 150 g), finely diced, or equivalent weight in chicken mince

1 small zucchini (100 g), finely diced

¼ cup medium-grain rice

¼ cup sultanas

Modelled on the fruity curries of yesteryear, this mild chicken curry can be made using almost any vegetable and is a great way to start your bub's love affair with all things curry and coconut. It is great with cauliflower, peas and potatoes — either instead of, or as well as, what's listed here. If you're adding more veggies just keep an eye on the amount of liquid during cooking as you may need to add more. All veggies should be diced to about 1 cm, or as small as you can manage. If you are going to puree you can make your dice bigger and vary cooking times as required.

Place the apple in a microwave-safe jug with a lid and microwave for 3 minutes until soft (or cook on the stovetop). Mash with a fork and set aside.

Meanwhile, heat the oil in a heavy-based saucepan and sauté the onion for 5 minutes until translucent. Add the garlic and curry powder and stir for 1 minute. Add the pumpkin, stock and coconut milk. Bring to the boil, then reduce the heat and simmer for 10 minutes.

Add the remaining ingredients, including the apple. Simmer covered for 15 minutes until thick, stirring regularly.

Remove from the heat and leave to rest for 10 minutes. Any excess liquid should be absorbed. Puree to the desired consistency, or leave as is. Divide into portions and freeze.

tip Try gently roasting the pumpkin first to alter the flavour of this dish.

lamb tagine

Age: fourth month of eating, plus

Suitable for freezing

Makes: 1½ cups

Prep time: 5 minutes

Cooking time: 15 minutes

1 tablespoon olive oil

½ onion, diced

½ teaspoon minced garlic

½ teaspoon minced ginger

¼ teaspoon ground turmeric or saffron

½ teaspoon ground cinnamon

½ teaspoon ground coriander

¼ teaspoon ground paprika

1 cup salt-reduced chicken stock

125 g minced lamb (you can add it frozen)

1 tomato, peeled and diced (you can leave the seeds in)

3 prunes with pips removed, chopped

⅓ cup couscous

⅓ cup water

Although 'tagine' is actually the name of the conical pot in which the casserole is cooked, and the dish tends to be slow-cooked, I'm happily borrowing the term in relation to the flavours and ingredients used. This cheat's version is a breeze to make and introduces your baby to a range and depth of flavours you just don't find in your typical meat-and-three-veg offering. And I love that it's so easy.

Heat a medium saucepan over low heat. Add the oil and onion and sauté for 5 minutes. Add the garlic, ginger and ground spices and cook for 1 minute.

Add the stock and mince and simmer for 10 minutes with a lid on. Add the tomato, prunes, couscous and a ⅓ cup of water, and return to a simmer.

Cook covered for 3 minutes, stirring occasionally. You should be left with a super-tasty wet mince and couscous casserole.

What your baby doesn't eat in one sitting can be served the following day or enjoyed by you. Freeze any leftovers in individual portions.

For a variation on this recipe, use veggies such as sweet potato, pumpkin or eggplant, which are all typical of Moroccan cooking. Dice or grate them as small as you can and add with the mince. Check to ensure they are cooked before adding the couscous.

pasta carbonara

Age: fifth month of eating,
plus (if egg-friendly)

Not suitable for freezing

Makes: 1 generous serve

Prep time: 2 minutes

Cooking time: 10 minutes

¼ cup dried soup pasta or other small
pasta shape (about ½–1 cup cooked
pasta if using leftovers)

¼ cup frozen peas

1 egg

2 teaspoons ricotta cheese

Generous sprinkling of shaved
parmesan cheese

Carbonara is traditionally made with an egg-and-oil base as opposed to cream, so this version is more akin to the original than you may think. It's super quick if you have the bits and pieces on hand from another meal and easy-peasy to make from scratch.

Cook the pasta and peas according to packet directions. Drain.

Place a room-temperature egg in a small saucepan and cover with cold water. Set your timer for 10 minutes, place the saucepan over medium heat and bring to the boil. When the timer goes off you should have a perfect hard-boiled egg. Remove from the heat and allow to cool before peeling.

In a good-sized bowl, mash the ricotta and egg together with a fork. Stir in the cooked pasta, cooked peas and parmesan.

For variations on this recipe, swap the peas for the Grated Carrot and Zucchini veggie mix from page 79 (this adds colour and sweetness). Sautéed mushrooms also work brilliantly. Use 2–3 button mushrooms, finely chopped and sautéed with a small amount of butter. As your baby gets older, consider adding some finely chopped ham to any of the veggie combinations.

> *tip* It's always handy to have a boiled egg on hand so why not cook a few and store them in the fridge for up to a few days? They make great snacks or handy sandwich fillings.

pappa pomodoro [italian bread soup]

Age: fifth month of eating, plus

Not suitable for freezing

Makes: 2½ cups

Prep time: 10 minutes

Cooking time: 20 minutes

1 tablespoon olive oil, plus extra to serve

2½ cm-piece carrot, peeled and grated (optional)

2½ cm-piece celery, peeled and finely diced (optional)

2½ cm-piece zucchini, grated (optional)

½ garlic clove, minced

½ a 425 g can (1 cup) diced tomatoes

¼ cup finely chopped fresh basil leaves, loosely packed

250 ml salt-reduced chicken stock

75 g day-old quality bread (do not use pre-sliced commercial bread)

¼ cup full-fat milk (optional, but it will soften the tomato flavour)

Grated parmesan cheese

The Italians are famous for creating masterpieces out of the simplest ingredients and this traditional bread soup is a prime example of simplicity at its best. I've adapted the original concept to include more vegetables, but these are optional if you prefer to be a purist.

Heat the olive oil in a saucepan and sauté the vegetables for 5 minutes. Add the garlic and cook for 1 minute. Add the tomatoes and cook for a few more minutes. Add the basil and stock and allow to simmer while preparing the bread.

Remove the crusts from the bread and cut it roughly into 1 cm cubes. Add to the pan, stir gently to combine and allow to simmer over the lowest possible heat for 20 minutes.

Remove from the heat and stir in the milk, if using.

Serve with a drizzle of olive oil and a sprinkle of parmesan.

> tip Double this recipe to create a super lunch or dinner for all the family. Mum and dad might like a little salt and pepper to really bring out the flavours.

chicken nuggets

Age: fifth month of eating, plus

Suitable for freezing

Makes: 24 nuggets

Prep time: 15 minutes

Cooking time: 15 minutes

1 slice brown or multigrain bread, diced (including crusts)

30 ml full-fat milk

100 g chicken mince or tenderloins

1 rasher of bacon (optional)

½ onion, finely diced

1 small garlic clove, minced

½ cup roughly chopped zucchini

¼ cup grated tasty cheese

1 egg

2 teaspoons cornflour

These delicious nuggets make great finger food and can be served with dips, diced veggies or just about anything you fancy. The use of the bread soaked in milk lightens the end result, making them particularly pleasing to babies who don't always seem to enjoy the texture or taste of meat. Being baked and not fried, they are much healthier than commercially prepared options. For older children you can replace the bread and milk with another 100 g of chicken.

Preheat the oven to 180°C. Line an oven tray with baking paper.

Soak the bread in the milk. Combine the chicken, bacon, onion, garlic and zucchini in a food processor and whiz for 10 seconds, scraping down the bowl and repeating if necessary.

Add the soaked bread, cheese, egg and cornflour and whiz for another 20 seconds until well combined.

Dollop teaspoonfuls of mixture onto the lined tray and bake in the oven for 10–15 minutes until starting to turn golden-brown.

Serve as finger food with your choice of veggies and accompaniments. Remaining nuggets can be frozen and thawed at your convenience.

risotto base

Age: fifth month of eating, plus

Suitable for freezing

Makes: 12 single-serve portions

Prep time: 2 minutes

Cooking time: 25 minutes

1 tablespoon olive or vegetable oil

1 onion, finely diced

1 garlic clove, minced

1 cup medium-grain rice

3 cups salt-reduced chicken or vegetable stock, hot

A true risotto is made using arborio rice and cooked lovingly with lots of attention and stirring. Unfortunately, this is something that new parents just can't spend the time doing. Well, not me anyway. So I created a risotto base. It's easy and doesn't require me to stand and stir for 30 minutes. I can make lots, freeze portions and then simply create a variety of risottos as we go. It works really well and allows for lots of experimentation with flavour combos without too much heartache over lost hours at the stove, should it end up on the floor.

You'll need a heavy-based saucepan with a lid. Heat the oil in the pan over medium heat, add the onion and sauté for 5 minutes. Add the garlic and cook for a further minute. Turn up to high, add the rice and stir constantly for about 3 minutes until the rice is coated with oil and some grains are starting to turn white. Turn the heat to the lowest possible setting and add the hot stock all in one go (stand back, it might splatter). Cover. After 15 minutes, check and stir well. Depending on how low you can get the heat, it will take somewhere between 15 and 25 minutes. The rice should be soft and a tad sticky.

When cool, the base is ready for portioning and freezing. About ¼ cup cooked risotto base will make a generous serve when your risotto is finished. You'll need to defrost each serve before you transform it into a risotto, preferably at room temperature but in the microwave is OK too.

Over the following pages you'll find a selection of delicious and nutritious risottos, but be creative and add your own flair.

> tip I use the snack-size snap-lock bags for freezing portions as they don't take up much room and can fit into nooks and crannies.

popeye risotto

Age: fifth month of eating, plus

Suitable for freezing

Makes: one portion

Prep time: 2 minutes

Cooking time: 3 minutes

1 portion risotto base (page 101)

1–2 handfuls baby spinach leaves, washed and chopped, or 1 cube Spinach Puree (page 78)

2 teaspoons butter

2 teaspoons ricotta cheese

Grated parmesan cheese

Remove the risotto base from the freezer and thaw at room temperature or in the microwave.

Place the spinach in a microwave-safe jug with a drop of water and microwave for 20 seconds. Melt the butter in a saucepan, add the thawed risotto base and stir well. When warm, remove from the heat, stir in the spinach and cheeses and serve.

borlotti bean risotto

Age: fifth month of eating, plus

Suitable for freezing

Makes: one portion

Prep time: 2 minutes

Cooking time: 3 minutes

1 portion risotto base (page 101)

¼ can borlotti beans, drained and rinsed (the remainder can make a great addition to a salad for mum and dad)

2 teaspoons butter

Grated parmesan cheese

1 teaspoon chopped fresh parsley or sage leaves

Remove the risotto base from the freezer and thaw at room temperature or in the microwave.

Roughly mash the beans. Melt the butter in a saucepan, add the herbs and stir for 30 seconds. Add the mashed beans, stirring to warm through. Add the thawed risotto and stir well. When warm, remove from the heat, stir in the cheese and serve.

spring veg risotto

Age: fifth month of eating, plus

Suitable for freezing

Makes: one portion

Prep time: 2 minutes

Cooking time: 3 minutes

1 portion risotto base (page 101)

Choose a selection of at least three vegetables to make up about ¼ cup (try a mix of asparagus, peas, spinach, zucchini or baby broad beans)

2 teaspoons butter

Grated parmesan cheese

1 teaspoon chopped fresh parsley leaves

Remove the risotto base from the freezer and thaw at room temperature or in the microwave.

Finely chop and microwave-steam your chosen vegetables. Melt the butter in a saucepan, add the risotto base and stir to warm. Combine with the cooked vegetables, cheese and parsley and serve.

pork sausage risotto

Age: fifth month of eating, plus

Suitable for freezing

Makes: one portion

Prep time: 2 minutes

Cooking time: 5 minutes

1 portion risotto base (page 101)

2 teaspoons butter

1 small tomato (50 g), peeled, deseeded and chopped (deseeding optional)

1 small pork sausage (chipolatas are great), filling squeezed out into a bowl and broken up with a fork

Grated parmesan cheese

2 fresh basil leaves, finely sliced (optional)

Remove the risotto base from the freezer and thaw at room temperature or in the microwave.

Melt the butter in a saucepan and cook off the sausage meat, breaking up with a spoon as you go. Add the tomato and cook for 2 minutes until starting to soften but not broken down. Add the risotto base and stir to combine. When warm, remove from the heat, stir in the cheese and basil and serve.

pumpkin and sage risotto

Age: fifth month of eating, plus

Suitable for freezing

Makes: one portion

Prep time: 2 minutes

Cooking time: 3 minutes

1 portion risotto base (page 101)

¼ cup roasted pumpkin pieces (page 79)

4 sage leaves, finely chopped (or ¼ teaspoon dried sage)

1 tablespoon butter

Grated parmesan cheese

Remove the risotto base from the freezer and thaw at room temperature or in the microwave.

Melt the butter in a saucepan, add the sage leaves and cook for 1 minute. Remove from the heat, add the pumpkin pieces and mash lightly with a fork.

Add the risotto base to the sage and pumpkin, return to the heat and stir to combine, adding a little extra water as necessary. Warm through, stir in the parmesan and serve.

chicken and roast capsicum risotto

Age: fifth month of eating, plus

Suitable for freezing

Makes: one portion

Prep time: 2 minutes

Cooking time: 5 minutes

1 portion risotto base (page 101)

1 chicken tenderloin
(or leftover roast chicken, about ¼ cup)

¼ cup finely diced roasted capsicum pieces (available from delis or roast them yourself and use leftovers in a salad)

2 teaspoons butter

Grated parmesan cheese

Remove the risotto base from the freezer and thaw at room temperature or in the microwave.

Poach the chicken tenderloin by placing it in a small saucepan and just covering with cold water. Bring to the boil and turn off immediately. Remove from the heat and allow to sit for 5 minutes. Remove from the water and dice or shred with two forks.

Melt the butter in a saucepan, add the risotto base and stir to heat, adding a little extra water as necessary. When warm, combine with the chicken, capsicum and parmesan and serve.

baby stroganoff

Age: fifth month of eating, plus

Suitable for freezing

Makes: 2 cups

Prep time: 10 minutes

Cooking time: 25 minutes

1 tablespoon plain flour

1 teaspoon paprika

200 g beef rump or eye fillet steak, trimmed of fat and gristle

2 tablespoons olive oil

1½ tablespoons butter

1 cup finely sliced button mushrooms

1 spring onion, trimmed and finely sliced

1 cup salt-reduced beef stock

1 tablespoon tomato paste

1 teaspoon Worcestershire sauce

1 tablespoon sour cream

1 tablespoon chopped fresh parsley leaves

Cooked pasta shapes or rice, to serve

A 1970s classic lives on. Great with rice or pasta and packed full of flavour, your bub is sure to love this version of 'the strog'. However, getting the meat super tender is key. No one likes chewy meat, especially not little ones, so vent your frustrations on an unsuspecting rump steak and you should end up with meltingly good beef slivers, all buttery and golden.

Combine the flour and paprika in a bowl. Lay the meat between two sheets of greaseproof paper. Belt, bash and tenderise the meat until thin and breaking down (I use a rolling pin). Roll into a log and thinly slice. Toss in the flour blend, separating with your fingers as you go.

Heat a non-stick frying pan over medium–high heat and add half the oil and butter. When foaming, brown the meat for 2 minutes, tossing occasionally. Remove the meat with a slotted spoon and place in a bowl.

Add the remaining oil and butter to the same pan. When bubbling, add the mushrooms and spring onion, turn the heat down to medium and caramelise for a few minutes. Stir occasionally and ensure you scrape up any of the tasty brown bits at the bottom of the pan before they burn. Add the stock, tomato paste and Worcestershire sauce and bring to the boil.

Reduce the heat, add the sour cream and warm through. Return the meat and juices to the pan with the parsley and warm through. Serve with cooked pasta or rice.

The stroganoff can be pureed to the desired consistency or left whole and eaten messily as finger food.

multigrain chicken bites

Age: sixth month of eating, plus

Suitable for freezing

Makes: 2 serves

Prep time: 5 minutes

Cooking time: 5 minutes

Multigrain crumb (makes about 1½ cups)

½ cup rolled oats

½ cup breadcrumbs

1 tablespoon linseeds (flaxseeds)

1 tablespoon sesame seeds

Chicken

1–2 chicken tenderloins per serve

2 teaspoons plain full-fat yoghurt

1–2 tablespoons multigrain crumb

1–2 tablespoons vegetable oil for frying

Steamed veggies, to serve

I was surprised how long it took for my children to take to chicken. Unless it was pureed or minced, they tended to eat around the meat. I'd thought that as chicken was so mild and breast meat was so pure, it would make a perfect baby food. But, alas, no. It took me an embarrassingly long time to realise it was the texture causing the grief, and once I started to tenderise the meat, their little teeth (or gums) could manage it much better.

Multigrain crumb Whiz the oats in a blender or grinder to make a coarse powder. Add to the breadcrumbs and mix in the linseeds and sesame seeds. Store in an airtight container.

Chicken Lay the chicken tenderloins between two pieces of greaseproof paper and pound them with a heavy object (rolling pin, tin of tomatoes, base of a saucepan) to flatten and break up the flesh. Cut into halves or thirds.

Smear yoghurt on both sides of the chicken pieces and then toss them in the crumb mixture, pressing to coat. Set aside.

Cover the base of a frying pan with a thin film of oil and heat over medium heat until a breadcrumb starts to sizzle and brown when dropped into the pan. Now cook the chicken pieces for a couple of minutes on each side until golden-brown. Remove and drain on clean absorbent paper. Serve with steamed veggies.

Cooked chicken bites can be frozen and reheated for quick meals or snacks.

> tip A traditional egg wash can be used in place of yoghurt, but using yoghurt means that egg-intolerant babies can also enjoy these bites.

fish pie

Age: fifth month of eating, plus

Suitable for freezing

Makes: 1½ cups filling

Prep time: 10 minutes

Cooking time: 15 minutes

200 g white fish (e.g. basa or rockling), skin and bones removed

1 cup full-fat milk

50 g broccoli pieces

2 hard-boiled eggs

1 small potato per serve, mashed (steam, boil or microwave the potato until soft and then fork-mash with a little butter and milk)

Grated tasty cheese

White sauce

1 tablespoon butter

2 teaspoons plain flour

I love good old-fashioned fish pie. It reminds me of English pubs on freezing cold days and pints of beer. So tasty and so hearty, we really should be eating them more often. You'll need to ensure your baby is OK with egg before you try this one, or just omit the boiled egg.

Preheat the oven to 180°C.

Place the fish and milk in a small saucepan, bring to the boil and simmer for 3 minutes. Remove the fish, flake and set aside. Reserve the milk. Steam or microwave the broccoli until tender but still bright green. Chop finely. Peel and finely chop the eggs and add to the reserved fish along with broccoli.

To make the white sauce, melt the butter in a saucepan, add the flour and cook, stirring, for 2 minutes. Add the reserved milk and stir rapidly to ensure no lumps form, whisking if you have to. Cook for a few minutes while stirring until the sauce starts to thicken. Add to the fish mix and stir thoroughly to combine.

Spoon into buttered ramekins and top with your pre-prepared potato mash and a sprinkling of grated cheese. Bake in the oven for 15 minutes until the cheese is melted and the pie is bubbling.

Freeze left-over pie filling in ice cube trays or silicone muffin pans. Now you can make pies to order by removing 2 or 3 cubes of pie filling and topping with fresh mashed potato.

tip Try a blend of white fish and salmon for something different.

fish fingers

Age: fifth month of eating, plus

Suitable for freezing

Makes: 4 servings

Prep time: 10 minutes

Cooking time: 5 minutes

2–4 teaspoons plain flour

1 cup breadcrumbs or multigrain crumb
(see page 108)

1 egg

Dash of full-fat milk

2 fresh Basa fillets (Basa is perfect as
it is cheap, readily available and has no
bones; otherwise, ask your fishmonger
to recommend a mild fish with no bones),
cut into smallish pieces (I usually get 5 or 6
from each fillet)

1 tablespoon butter

1 tablespoon olive oil

Steamed potatoes, to serve

Tartare sauce, to serve

These simple fish fingers are an ideal finger food and
will no doubt continue to be a favourite for many years
to come. Warning: make extra because you'll be eating
them, too!

To crumb the fish, place the flour on one plate and the
breadcrumbs on another. Crack the egg into a small bowl and
lightly whisk with a dash of milk or water.

Lightly coat each piece of fish with flour, dusting off any excess.
Then dip each piece in the egg mix and cover with breadcrumbs,
pressing them on firmly. Rest the fish on a clean plate while you
prepare the remaining pieces (prepared fish can be refrigerated
or frozen at this point).

To cook the fish, heat a frying pan and add half the butter and
oil. Heat until foaming. Cook the fish in two batches, turning
after a few minutes and adding the rest of the butter and oil as
needed. Each side should be golden-brown, but don't make it too
crunchy for little ones. Remove from the pan and allow to cool.

Fish fingers are great served with steamed potatoes and
tartare sauce.

tip Cooked fish can also be frozen. I tend to freeze it cooked as it's so
easy to heat in the microwave.

lasagne

Age: fifth month of eating, plus

Suitable for freezing

Makes: 1 dish – about 8 serves, depending on who is eating it

Prep time: 20 minutes

Cooking time: 40 minutes

200 g butternut pumpkin, peeled and diced

1 zucchini (150 g), sliced lengthways into 5 mm-thick slices

2 tablespoons olive oil

150 g baby spinach, washed and dried

1 quantity Cheesy Sauce (page 80)

1 quantity Bolognaise for Little People (page 60)

4–6 dried lasagne sheets (depending on the size of your dish and the sheets)

Extra grated cheese for topping

Sometimes I wish I were Garfield. Is there anything better than a good lasagne? This version is loaded with extra veggies but of course you can leave them out if you're a bit of a traditionalist. Feel free to double or triple the recipe while you're at it.

Preheat the oven to 180°C. Line a baking tray with baking paper.

Toss the pumpkin and zucchini in olive oil and place on the baking tray. Roast for 20–30 minutes until soft and yummy and set aside.

Heat a frying pan, add the spinach and a sprinkling of water and stir and toss with tongs. The spinach will cook down to almost nothing in a matter of minutes. Remove and set aside.

While the veggies are roasting, prepare (or defrost!) the Cheesy Sauce (page 80) and Bolognaise for Little People (page 60).

To assemble the lasagne Smear some bolognaise sauce over the bottom of a suitably sized baking dish – about 20 cm square. Cover with a layer of lasagne sheets. Next, spoon over a layer of bolognaise sauce topped with a layer of zucchini slices (they don't need to be perfect) and a drizzle of cheese sauce. Repeat with a layer of pasta sheets, the remaining bolognaise, the roasted pumpkin and the spinach. Pour on all of the remaining cheese sauce and spread out evenly. Cover with foil and bake for 30 minutes. Remove the foil, sprinkle with a handful of grated tasty cheese and return to the oven for 15–20 minutes.

Allow to cool. Cut into slices and serve to your baby. Remaining slices can be frozen in individual containers.

mac 'n' cheese

Age: fifth month of eating, plus

Suitable for freezing

Makes: 2 cups

Prep time: 10 minutes

Cooking time: 15 minutes

½ cup dried macaroni

1 cup Cheesy Veg (page 80)

2 teaspoons breadcrumbs

¼ cup grated tasty cheese

2 teaspoons butter

This is a great recipe as it features loads of hidden veggies!

Preheat the oven to 180°C.

Cook the macaroni according to packet instructions. Meanwhile, prepare the Cheesy Veg if you don't have any in the freezer.

Combine the breadcrumbs and tasty cheese in a bowl. Set aside.

Combine the cooked macaroni and Cheesy Veg and stir well. Spoon into a buttered oven-proof dish or ramekins and sprinkle over the breadcrumbs. Dollop a teaspoon of butter on each and bake in the oven for 15 minutes.

Serve with steamed greens if you wish, but be happy in the knowledge that there are loads of veggies already buried in this classic dish.

Remaining portions can be frozen in individual containers.

tip For added flavour, add a small can of tuna or salmon (bones removed).

beef burgers

Age: fifth month of eating, plus
(if egg-friendly)

Suitable for freezing

Makes: 1 cup burger mix or 24 burgers

Prep time: 15 minutes

Cooking time: 10 minutes

1 slice wholemeal or multigrain bread, diced (including crusts)

30 ml full-fat milk

1 tablespoon olive oil

½ onion, finely diced

½ garlic clove, minced

½ cup grated zucchini

½ cup grated carrot

100 g beef mince

4 kalamata olives with pips removed, chopped (optional, but a great way to extend your baby's palate)

1 egg

A few finely chopped fresh parsley leaves

2 teaspoons grated parmesan cheese

We Aussies love a burger and this is a great way to get your little one off and racing. A soft non-meaty texture makes these beef burgers easy for babies and oven-baking them is quick and simple. Serve them with your own burgers to make your baby really feel a part of the family.

Preheat the oven to 180°C. Line an oven tray with baking paper.

Soak the bread in the milk. Meanwhile, heat half the oil in a frying pan and sauté the onion, garlic, zucchini and carrot for 8 minutes until softened. Remove from the heat and allow to cool slightly.

In a separate bowl, combine the mince, soaked bread, olives (if using), egg, parsley, parmesan and the remaining oil. Add the cooled vegetables and mix thoroughly with your hands. If you have a food processor, simply add all ingredients and pulse a few times to combine, but do not mince too finely.

Dollop teaspoons of the mixture onto the oven tray. Cook for 10 minutes. Serve as finger food with your choice of sides.

Remaining burgers can be frozen and thawed at your convenience.

tip To ensure burgers are easy to get out of the freezer, package separately in small quantities (snap-lock bags are great).

quesadillas

Age: fifth month of eating, plus

Not suitable for freezing

Makes: 1 generous serve

Prep time: 2 minutes

Cooking time: 3 minutes

2 small flour tortillas (or 1 large one, cut in half)

2 teaspoons refried beans*

¼ cup grated tasty cheese

Chopped fresh coriander leaves (optional)

* Available in the Mexican section of your supermarket.

Quesadillas, you ask? They're kind of like a Mexican toasted sandwich. You can play with the fillings and toast them either flat or rolled-up – whatever works best for you and your baby.

Spread one tortilla with refried beans. Sprinkle with cheese and dot with coriander leaves. Top with the remaining tortilla and toast in a flat sandwich press or a dry frying pan, cooking each side for about 2 minutes until the cheese has melted. Cut into small wedges and allow to cool before serving.

Avocado mashed with plain yoghurt makes a great accompaniment as a dip. Mild taco sauce is another way to extend your baby's palate when they're ready.

For variations, add grated carrot and/or finely chopped steamed broccoli. Otherwise, you can try sweet corn and cheese. Baked beans and cheese is another option, although these ones can be a bit messy!

> *tip* When you open your pack of tortillas, pull them all out and separate each one with a small square of baking paper. Return them to the pack, seal with tape and freeze. This will allow you to remove just one or two tortillas at a time without them sticking and tearing. Tortillas also make a handy pram snack as a biscuit alternative and they come in a great multigrain variety.

real baked beans

Age: fifth month of eating

Not suitable for freezing

Makes: 2 cups

Prep time: 2 minutes

Cooking time: 3 minutes

1 tablespoon olive oil

1 small onion, finely diced

1 bay leaf

1 rasher of rindless bacon, diced

1 garlic clove, crushed

Pinch of chilli powder (go on, be daring!)

¼ teaspoon ground cumin powder

¼ teaspoon mustard powder

1 × 425 g can cannellini beans

2 teaspoons Worcestershire sauce

1 tablespoon cider vinegar

2 teaspoons brown sugar

½ can crushed tomatoes

Chopped fresh parsley leaves

While I definitely don't scoff at canned baked beans – I love them – they really don't compare to these ones, which are made with love, lots of flavour and a whole lot less sugar and salt. Give them a try. They also make a delicious breakfast on toast for the rest of the family.

Heat the oil in a saucepan over medium heat and sauté the onion and bay leaf for 5 minutes.

Add the bacon, garlic and spices and cook for another 5 minutes.

Add the cannellini beans, Worcestershire sauce, vinegar, sugar and tomatoes. Simmer for 30 minutes. Allow to cool a little.

Serve on their own sprinkled with fresh parsley, or with steamed potatoes or toast.

fried rice

1 egg

1 tablespoon vegetable oil

1 rasher (25 g) short-cut bacon

1 small spring onion, white part only,
finely sliced

¼ teaspoon minced garlic

¼ teaspoon minced ginger

¼ cup frozen peas

¼ cup canned or frozen corn kernels

¼ cup finely diced carrot

½ cup cooked rice

1 tablespoon light soy sauce (use less if you
don't have the light variety as it will be
too strong)

Fun, colourful and messy to eat! Make sure you've got the
drop sheet out for this one. This is a great meal to make
when you have some leftover boiled rice or cook some
especially – you can freeze leftovers to have on standby.

In a small bowl, whisk together the egg with a tablespoon
of water.

Heat half the oil in a frying pan and, when hot, add the egg
and cook it like an omelette. Remove and set aside to cool, then
thinly slice.

Add the remaining oil to the pan and cook the bacon for
1 minute. Add the spring onion, garlic, ginger, peas, corn and
carrot and cook for a further minute.

Add the rice and cook for another minute, stirring well.
Add the soy and cook for 1 minute. Toss the egg slices through.
Serve and enjoy.

tip As your baby gets older, try adding lap cheong (Chinese pork sausage).
These are readily available in the Asian section of supermarkets and
impart a lovely smoky flavour. Finely slice half of the sausage and add
it with the bacon.

zucchini slice

Age: sixth month of eating, plus
(if egg- friendly)

Suitable for freezing

Makes: 20 cm square baking dish

Prep time: 5 minutes

Cooking time: 30 minutes

2 zucchini (about 250 g), grated

1–2 rashers (50 g) rindless bacon,
finely chopped

½ small onion (50 g), finely chopped

½ cup grated tasty cheese

½ cup self-raising flour

2 tablespoons olive oil

3 eggs

I have my friend Amber to thank for this one. She makes the best zucchini slice going around and kindly shared her recipe with me. This is a slightly altered version for your bub to enjoy, but I guarantee you will love it, too. Thanks, Amber.

Preheat the oven to 180°C. Butter and line a 20 cm square (or round) cake or slice tin.

Combine the zucchini, bacon, onion and cheese in a bowl.

In another bowl, add the flour, oil and eggs, mixing well. Combine with the zucchini mixture and pour into the tin.

Bake for 25–30 minutes until set and starting to colour.

Allow to cool in the tin before turning out and cutting. Slices can be frozen and thawed as required.

tip Substitute some of the zucchini for grated pumpkin and/or carrot for a sweeter vegetable slice.

snacks and on the go

Clean and easy food for the pram or car is essential.
Never leave home without some packed in your
bag. These options are great as snacks or meals in
themselves — packed with invisible veggies, protein
and general yumminess, they are easy to prepare and
freeze brilliantly.

Serve the following dishes as meals in themselves, or as part of
a spread including additional vegetables, dips and cheese pieces.

savoury muffins

Age: fifth month of eating, plus
(if egg-friendly)

Suitable for freezing

Makes: 12 big or 24 mini muffins

Prep time: 5 minutes

Cooking time: 15 minutes

Butter or oil for greasing

1¼ cups (170 g) plain flour

1½ teaspoons baking powder

1 cup grated veggies (I like carrot and zucchini)

50 g ham, finely chopped

1 cup grated tasty cheese

¾ cup full-fat milk

1 egg

50 g butter, melted

Muffins are good for lunches, snacks, parties, picnics, finger food, the car, the lunchbox and, best of all, the freezer. Why wouldn't you always have a batch on hand?

Preheat the oven to 180°C and grease the muffin tins. I find the easiest way is to use a spray oil to give a light coating. Alternatively, melt some additional butter and use a pastry brush to get into all the holes.

Place the dry ingredients in a mixing bowl and whisk lightly with a balloon whisk to aerate and combine well. Add the grated veggies, ham and cheese. Using your fingers, lightly toss and mix through to separate and evenly distribute the ingredients.

In another bowl, whisk together the milk, egg and melted butter. Add the wet ingredients to the dry ones. Stir lightly until just combined — do not overwork or the muffins will be tough.

Spoon the mixture into the muffin tins. Cook mini muffins for 15 minutes and larger ones for 25 minutes.

Allow to cool in the tin for 5 minutes before removing to a cooling rack. Eat there and then or keep them in the fridge for a few days, giving them a quick zap in the microwave to freshen them up. Alternatively, freeze in snap-lock bags and enjoy any time.

Other combinations (instead of, or as well as, the above listed ingredients):

* Fresh herbs or chives.

* Grated pumpkin or sweet potato and corn, (or all of them).

* Semi-dried tomato and feta (yes, my babies love feta).

* Roasted red capsicum, spinach and ham.

* Antipasto — buy a tub of antipasto mix from your deli and chop it all up (be sure to remove any pips if there are olives in the mix).

* Get creative — think of your favourite pizza toppings and know that just about anything will work.

french toast

Age: fourth month of eating, plus
(if egg-friendly)

Not suitable for freezing

Makes: Makes 2 serves

Prep time: 1 minute

Cooking time: 4 minutes

1 egg

A dash of full-fat milk

A dash of Tabasco sauce (optional)

2 slices wholemeal or multigrain bread

1 tablespoon butter

French toast is our standard 'in a hurry' breakfast. I can prepare it quickly and my kids are happy to sit up in the pram or car with a little bowl and munch their breakfast while we get from A to B. Perfect for creche days or any early start. It even works well made the night before and just heated through in the microwave in the morning.

Lightly whisk the egg, milk and Tabasco (if using) together in a bowl. Pour into a dish large enough to hold 2 slices of bread flat with no overlapping. Submerge the bread slices in the egg mix and turn once or twice until bread has soaked up all the egg.

Heat a non-stick frying pan (large enough to hold the two pieces of bread) over medium heat, add the butter and when starting to foam carefully transfer the bread to the pan. Cook each side for about 2 minutes until starting to turn golden. Remove from the pan and cut into small pieces. You do not need to remove the crusts as they will be soft.

Microwave This version definitely doesn't taste as good as the original but it's fine if you're in a rush (and let's face it, best laid plans can easily go astray with little ones). My kids certainly don't discriminate between the pan-fried or microwave version.

Use the same ingredients as above but start by melting the butter in a microwave-safe dish large enough to hold the bread slices. Crack the egg into same dish and whisk with the butter and a little milk. Add the bread slices and submerge, turning once or twice. Return to the microwave and cook for 1 minute. Turn and cook for another minute.

For variations on this recipe, grate a little tasty cheese onto the bread once you have cooked the first side. The residual heat will melt the cheese. Otherwise, I discovered that leftover Vegemite sandwiches work great dipped in the egg mix and pan-fried.

sweet corn fritters

Age: fifth month of eating, plus
(if egg-friendly)

Suitable for freezing

Makes: about 20 fritters

Prep time: 2 minutes

Cooking time: 5 minutes

1 egg

1 cup self-raising flour

1 × 310 g can creamed corn

¼ cup full-fat milk

Butter for cooking

So easy and versatile, these are a real favourite in our home. The basic version is most suitable for gummy babies, but you can easily adapt it for a wider variety of flavours and textures.

Whisk the egg in a medium-sized bowl. Sift in the flour and add the corn and milk. Mix well with a fork.

Melt 2 teaspoons of butter in a frying pan over medium–low heat. Gently drop spoonfuls of the batter into the pan and allow to cook for a couple of minutes each side until golden-brown. Remove the fritters from the pan and rest on absorbent paper. Repeat the process until all the batter is used.

Serve either on their own, as a snack or diced as a vegetable accompaniment. We love them with sausages or smoked salmon. Fritters can wrapped in foil or small snap-lock bags, frozen and then quickly re-heated in the microwave as needed.

Variations:

Corn and pea fritters: Add ¼ cup cooked peas to the batter.

Corn and feta fritters: Substitute a 375 g can whole corn kernels (strained) for the creamed corn, adding ¼ cup milk and 50 g crumbled feta to the mix.

Vegetable fritters: Add ½ cup steamed diced veggies to the base recipe. Try potato, pumpkin and/or zucchini.

Fresh corn fritters: Remove kernels from fresh corn cobs and microwave on high in a microwave-safe dish with a dash of water for 4 minutes. Strain and add to the batter along with ¼ cup milk and a dash of paprika.

> *tip* A few fresh chopped chives or spring onions add some zing to all of the above variations.

mini frittatas

Age: fifth month of eating, plus
(if egg-friendly)

Suitable for freezing

Makes: about 12 mini frittatas

Prep time: 4 minutes

Cooking time: 10 minutes

2 eggs

4 teaspoons ricotta cheese

¼ cup grated tasty cheese

2 cubes Grated Carrot and Zucchini
(page 79), thawed if necessary

½ cup cooked rice or Risotto Base
(page 101), thawed if necessary

Mini muffin pans allow you to make a great mini frittata
that little hands can easily manage. There is really no end of
variations for these. This recipe makes use of the veggie bases
you are likely to have in the freezer, which means it's super
simple to whip up a batch.

Preheat the oven to 200°C. Grease a mini muffin pan with a
spray of cooking oil.

In a medium-sized bowl, whisk the eggs. Add the ricotta and
cheese and stir to combine. Add the veggies and rice and stir.
Spoon into the mini muffin pan and cook for 10 minutes. Allow to
cool in the pan.

Serve warm or cold.

For variations on this recipe, try ham/cheese/tomato, steamed
potato cubes and spinach, salmon and broccoli, or tuna and corn.

pikelets

Age: fifth month of eating, plus

Suitable for freezing

Makes: 15

Prep time: 2 minutes

Cooking time: 5 minutes

¼ cup sugar

2 eggs

¾ cup full-fat milk

1 teaspoon baking powder

1½ cups self-raising flour

Butter for frying

This is my Nana's recipe, exactly as it appears in her handwriting in my Mum's cherished notebook of recipes. It's a classic – so delicious and so easy. I have fond memories of crowding around Mum's bright-orange electric frying pan in the late '70s cooking these, eagerly awaiting for the bubbles to pop before we could flip them. You'll love them and so will your baby.

According to Nana: 'Beat sugar and eggs well. Add milk, then dry ingredients. Fry in pan with butter.'

Nana's instructions are brief but it really is that simple. Use a non-stick frying pan over medium heat and spoon the batter into the pan, waiting for each pikelet to set and bubbles to appear and then pop before turning. They can be served plain or with butter and jam. Please note, it's OK to reduce the sugar to ¼ cup if you want, but I had to stay true to the original.

dinner [soups]

Following my premise of protein-based lunches and easy-to-eat dinners, thick soups continued to be a favourite dinner option for us. I think that a tasty, hearty bowl of soup is hard to pass by at any age and the fact that they are power-packed with goodness only makes them more valuable.

Start to play with texture and flavour combinations to extend your baby's eating ability and always serve with buttered toast soldiers or other finger food to help develop fine motor skills.

homestyle veg and barley soup

Age: fourth month of eating, plus

Suitable for freezing

Makes: 2 cups

Prep time: 10 minutes

Cooking time: 40 minutes

1 tablespoon olive oil

1 onion, finely diced

1 garlic clove, minced

1 carrot, finely diced

1 stick celery with stringy bits removed, finely diced

500 ml salt-reduced veggie stock

¼ cup pearl barley

1 tablespoon tomato paste

½ cup finely diced butternut pumpkin, (or 1 cube pumpkin puree if you don't mind not seeing the pieces)

1 small zucchini, finely diced

1 cob sweet corn, kernels removed

¾ cup frozen peas

I feel virtuous just cooking this, let alone eating it. You know you are giving your baby nothing but goodness in this soup and it makes a great base to develop as your family grows. Simply add lamb shanks or beef shins along with the stock and simmer for an extra two hours and you'll have a hearty family meal.

Heat the oil in a saucepan and sauté the onion, garlic, carrot and celery for 5 minutes.

Add the stock, barley, tomato paste, pumpkin, zucchini and corn, bring to the boil and simmer for 30 minutes.

Add the peas and cook for another 5 minutes.

The soup should be thick and the veggies and barley soft. Blend to the desired texture or serve as is.

Any remaining soup can be frozen in portions.

tip Serving this soup with a teaspoon of ricotta or cottage cheese will help to bind it on your baby's spoon.

curried sweet potato soup

Age: fourth month of eating, plus

Suitable for freezing

Makes: 2½ cups

Prep time: 5 minutes

Cooking time: 25 minutes

1 tablespoon olive oil

1 tablespoon butter

1 onion, roughly chopped

1 garlic clove, minced

½ teaspoon curry powder

500 g sweet potato, peeled and roughly chopped

400 ml salt-reduced chicken stock

1 tablespoon apple puree (or use ½ peeled, cored and diced apple and add with stock)

Full-fat plain yoghurt, to serve

Fresh bread or buttered toast soldiers are a perfect accompaniment to any bowl of soup. Show your babies from an early age how to dip their bread in their soup and enjoy watching them engage in the process of feeding themselves. Messy but delicious!

Heat a saucepan over medium heat and add the oil and butter. Add the onion and sauté for 5 minutes. Add the garlic and curry powder and cook for 30 seconds.

Add the sweet potato and stock and cook for 20 minutes, or until the potato is soft. Add the apple puree and remove from the heat. Puree using a stick blender.

Serve with a dollop of plain yoghurt. Freeze any remaining soup in portions.

parsnip and potato soup

Age: fourth month of eating, plus

Suitable for freezing

Makes: 4 cups

Prep time: 10 minutes

Cooking time: 20 minutes

1 tablespoon olive oil

1 tablespoon butter

1 onion (100 g), roughly chopped

1 garlic clove, minced

½ teaspoon ground cumin

½ teaspoon ground coriander

300 g parsnip, peeled and roughly chopped

150 g potato, peeled and roughly chopped

300 ml salt-reduced chicken stock

100 ml full-fat milk

Chopped fresh parsley leaves

Love a root veggie? Then this one's for you.

Heat the oil and butter in a saucepan. Add the onion and sauté for 5 minutes. Add the garlic and the ground cumin and coriander and cook for 1 minute.

Add the parsnip, potato and stock and cook for 20 minutes, or until the veggies are tender.

Remove from the heat and puree using a stick blender, adding milk as you go to achieve a good consistency. You want it to be thick enough to hold on the spoon, to enable self-feeding.

Serve with fresh chopped parsley. Freeze any remaining soup in portions.

tip Thinly sliced chorizo, pan-fried and sprinkled on top, makes this a delicious dinner for mum and dad with some fresh crusty bread.

142

roasted cauliflower and chickpea soup

Age: fourth month of eating, plus

Suitable for freezing

Makes: 3 cups

Prep time: 5 minutes

Cooking time: 35 minutes

1 head of cauliflower (300 g), cut into florets

1 teaspoon fresh or ½ teaspoon dried thyme

2 tablespoons olive oil

1 onion, finely diced

1 garlic clove, minced

250 ml salt-reduced chicken stock

125 ml full-fat milk

1 cup canned chickpeas, drained and rinsed

A great power-packed dinner full of protein, veggies and dairy.

Preheat the oven to 180°C.

Toss the cauliflower and thyme in half the olive oil. Roast in the oven for 20–30 minutes until starting to turn golden. Do not allow to colour too much.

In a saucepan, heat the remaining olive oil and sweat the onion for 10 minutes. Add the garlic and cook for 1 minute. Add the roasted cauliflower and stock. Bring to the boil, then remove from the heat and add the milk and half the chickpeas.

Puree with a stick blender. The soup should be thick enough to hold on your baby's spoon. Garnish with a few whole or fork-crushed chickpeas for texture.

Any remaining soup can be frozen in portions.

tip Leftover whole chickpeas are great to serve on the side. Let your baby play with them as finger food.

desserts and drinks

Whether it's a comforting bowl of something delicious before bed or a tutti-frutti afternoon drink, it's great to know that what you are offering is delicious and nutritious.

I don't advocate serving dessert every night – the last thing you want is for your baby to expect it and even hold out for it! But it is nice to have a treat every once in a while. Try not to fall into the trap of offering dessert as a way of filling your babies up if they haven't eaten their main meal. This can reinforce the notion of holding out for sweets.

These drinks are handy supplements for bulking up milk intake or simply using up some excess fruit lingering in your bowl – catch it early, prepare and freeze fruit pieces and you have a ready supply of natural fruit drinks and puree bases.

I hope you and your babies get as much joy out these as we did (and still do!).

sleepy rice pudding

Age: fourth month of eating, plus

Suitable for freezing

Makes: 1 generous serve

Prep time: 1 minute

Cooking time: 5 minutes

¼ cup rice flakes (available in the health food section of your supermarket)

½ cup full-fat milk

½ teaspoon castor sugar

It's nice to spoil your baby. In winter, a warm and hearty rice pudding is a lovely way to end the day and head off to bed to sleep the night through. Well, we can only hope.

Combine all the ingredients in a saucepan and simmer over low heat for about 5 minutes, stirring occasionally.

The rice flakes will soften and you will end up with a porridge-like consistency.

For a variation, add 1 teaspoon of sultanas to the mix at the start of cooking, or omit the sugar and add 1 teaspoon of strawberry jam at the end of cooking, stirring thoroughly.

banana custard with toasted coconut

Age: fifth month of eating, plus

Not suitable for freezing

Makes: 2 serves

Prep time: 1 minute

Cooking time: 5 minutes

1 cup desiccated coconut, toasted
(you only need 1 teaspoon per serving but it makes sense to prepare a small quantity and store it in an airtight container so it's always on hand. It's delicious on muesli!)

½ cup full-fat milk

1 egg

1 teaspoon castor sugar

1 drop vanilla essence (optional)

½ ripe banana

If only I had a video of the first time my babies tried this dessert. They expressed a look of pure delight and then a 'Why have you been withholding this from us, Mum?' kind of a look, followed by a frenzy of hands and spoons. There was no question about including it in this book.

Heat the oven to 180°C and spread the coconut on a tray lined with baking paper. Roast for 5–6 minutes until golden, but keep an eye on it as it burns quickly. Remove from the oven and allow to cool before storing in a jar or airtight container.

Now gently warm the milk in the top of a double saucepan. In another bowl, lightly whisk the egg, sugar and vanilla (if using). Add to the warmed milk and continue to cook slowly over simmering water, stirring with a wooden spoon until the mixture coats the back of the spoon and leaves a trail behind it. Remove from the heat and allow to cool slightly. Mash the banana, add a teaspoon of the toasted coconut and stir in the cooled custard.

> tip You can prepare the custard before dinner but make sure you transfer it to a cool bowl (to ensure it doesn't keep cooking) and cover it tightly with plastic wrap. Also, do not cook custard on too high a heat or you will end up with scrambled eggs.

fruit whip

2 teaspoons frozen blueberries

2 cm-piece ripe banana

1 thin wedge of melon, rockmelon or watermelon, thick skin and seeds removed

100 ml mango juice or water

A dairy-free delicious dose of fibre that anyone of any age can enjoy. A great hot-day snack.

Place all the ingredients in a blender and whiz until smooth.

Pour into a cup and enjoy.

> tip If you have bananas starting to ripen too quickly, peel and chop them into 2-cm pieces, pack them into a container, separating layers with greaseproof paper, and freeze. They are great added to fruit drinks.

banana smoothie

½ ripe banana, peeled

100 ml full-fat milk

2 teaspoons full-fat plain yoghurt

1 drop vanilla essence

Sprinkle of ground cinnamon or nutmeg

I was devastated to discover that neither Sophie nor Louis seemed to like bananas initially, something I was desperate for them to enjoy. I watched longingly as my fellow parents happily offered their eager eaters bananas, the ultimate in transportable and healthy food. So one day, with a fruit bowl full of unwanted ageing bananas, I decided to make a smoothie. Well, did we discover a taste for bananas! A smoothie a day quickly led to multiple bananas being eaten on a daily basis. The banana craze has died down these days but the love affair with smoothies lives on. They make a great afternoon snack and if you have a non-eater, at least you know they are receiving a lot of goodness and energy from these power-packed drinks.

Place the banana in a blender or suitable canister for your stick blender. Add all the other ingredients and whiz till smooth. Easy.

Bananas are terrific as they are always available, but summer brings with it a super range of fruits that you can experiment with. For variations on this recipe, add a few blueberries along with the banana to make a mixed smoothie, or, omit the banana and use four fresh strawberries that have been washed and hulled, or, omit the banana and use a ripe mango cheek. Please note that honey is not recommended for babies under the age of 1. I found vanilla to be a great substitute for a mild sweetener and it also helped to add a flavour dimension that was otherwise missing.

baking for baby

I love a home-baked treat — who doesn't? Being the keen cook I am, I relished the idea of baking for my kids. For me, it conjured up images of times past, coming home from school to a steaming hot cinnamon teacake baked by Mum.

Hmmm ... if only I lived in the '50s, when the commercial reality of modern life was different.

Sleep times are a great time for baking for your baby. You get to feel all nurturing and loving and they get to enjoy a special treat when they wake up. Equally, these recipes are great for sharing with visitors, young and old, especially if you are hosting parents' groups or play dates.

strawberry muffins

Age: third month of eating, plus
(if egg-friendly)

Not suitable for freezing

Makes: 24 mini muffins

Prep time: 5 minutes

Cooking time: 15 minutes

220 g plain flour

2 teaspoons baking powder

100 g white sugar

¾ cup buttermilk

1 egg

¾ cup vegetable oil

¾ cup strawberries, washed, hulled and cut into small pieces

Surprisingly easy and delicious, these are great for a treat and even better to share with a group. Best made with super-tasty fresh strawberries (they're a great way to use up a punnet), these are also delicious made with any frozen berry.

Preheat the oven to 180°C. Grease and dust a 24-hole small muffin tin. I find the easiest way is to use a spray oil to give a light coating. Alternatively, melt some additional butter and use a pastry brush to get into all the holes. To dust, spoon a small amount of flour into each hole and tip, rotate and tap the tray around until the flour coats the muffin holes. This will prevent the natural sugars from the berries sticking and make it easier to remove the muffins.

Sift together the flour and baking powder. Add the sugar and combine. Whisk together the buttermilk, egg and oil and add to the dry ingredients, along with the strawberries. Stir very lightly to combine. Do not overwork or the muffins will be tough.

Spoon the mixture into the muffin tins and cook for 15 minutes.

Allow to cool in the tin for 5 minutes before removing to a cooling rack.

banana balls

Age: fifth month of eating, plus

Suitable for freezing

Makes: about 10 balls

Prep time: 5 minutes ·

Cooking time: 12 minutes

1 ripe banana, peeled

8 digestive biscuits, crushed to a
rustic crumb

1 teaspoon ground cinnamon

1 teaspoon castor sugar

One lucky baby will love you for these. Like a piece of cake in
a ball, they are clean to eat and extremely moreish. Great for
anyone with egg allergies.

Preheat the oven to 180°C.

Combine the biscuit crumbs, cinnamon and sugar.

Mash the banana very well. Stir in about ¾ of the biscuit
crumbs, reserving the rest to roll the balls in. The dough
should be soft and malleable but not too sticky – add more
crumbs if necessary. Roll teaspoonfuls of the mixture into balls
and gently toss in the remaining crumb mix to coat.

Place on a baking tray and bake for 10–12 minutes. Remove
and cool. The balls should be moist but not gooey. They're
best eaten the same day, but can be frozen and microwaved.

12 months plus

12 months plus

Most of the advice you'll receive suggests that all babies should be eating the family meal by now. While this might be fine for some, for many it is not. Do what works best for you and please don't feel badly if you are still preparing separate meals for your tot.

In our family, our love of Asian cuisines and all things spicy means our meals are often not appropriate for our kids. Little ones don't generally like tom yum soup. As one-year-olds, Sophie and Louis still had most of their meals specially prepared for them, much to the chagrin of my maternal health nurse. Having said that, I did not offer options. Cooking meals for them was enough work without indulging their new-found independence. At around 12–18 months they started to become fussier, so my best advice to you is to beware of options. As tempting as it might be, do not start letting your little one dictate what they will eat. I know of too many toddlers who have started turning their noses up at the main meal and demanding yoghurt or other favourites. Once you indulge them, it's all over. Be strong and let them know they will miss out.

Some toddlers really like to test their parents by hardly eat anything. If you have one of these, remember that in most cases children will not starve themselves and one way or another will get what they need. Serve your fussy toddler high-calorie meals and snacks (not junk food) and try to find a fail-safe meal you can serve regularly, such as cheesy scrambled eggs, pasta bolognaise or porridge with stewed fruit for breakfast. But if you have real concerns about their eating please consult your health professional.

Around this time you should also start to push the boundaries: increase spice, use more flavoursome ingredients such as olives, bacon and other strong foods, and experiment with texture and your own personal cooking style. Take the pressure off yourself a little and start to cut back on the cooked lunch and let the humble sandwich shine. Make sure you are having shared family mealtimes, if you haven't been already. If your family's schedule doesn't usually allow for mum and dad to sit at the table with bub, make sure you do so on weekends to expose them to the way you eat and share a meal. After all, it's all part of the experience.

muesli bars

Age: 12 months, plus

Makes: about 20 mini bars

Prep time: 15 minutes

Cooking time: none!

1½ cups rolled oats

½ cup desiccated coconut

½ cup sunflower seeds

½ cup sesame seeds

½ cup pumpkin seeds

⅓ cup linseeds (flaxseeds)

½ cup sultanas or dried cranberries (or a mix of both)

100 g butter – do not use butter substitutes

½ cup honey

¼ cup brown sugar

Simple to make and better tasting than any commercial ones I've come across, these muesli bars keep well and make a great snack. Remember that honey is not recommended for babies under the age of 1, due to the risk of infant botulism.

Line a 20 x 28 cm (approx.) slice tin with baking paper.

Combine the oats, coconut, sunflower, sesame and pumpkin seeds in a large frying pan and stir over medium heat for 5–7 minutes to toast. Remove from the heat and tip into a cold bowl to stop the toasting process. Add the linseeds and dried fruit.

In a separate saucepan, combine the butter, honey and brown sugar. Cook over medium heat for 3 minutes, stirring occasionally to allow the sugar to dissolve. Leave on the heat for a further 5 minutes without stirring. The mixture will bubble and start to caramelise. After 5 minutes, take a small teaspoon of the mixture and drop it into a bowl of cold water – it should form soft, caramelly balls. If not, leave for another 30 seconds and test again. The consistency is important as this will determine how crumbly or chewy your slice is.

Remove from the heat and pour over the muesli mix. Stir well and spread the mixture into the slice tin, pressing down well with the back of a metal spatula. Allow to set for a few hours. Remove from the tin and, using a sharp knife, cut into bars. Store in an airtight container in the fridge for up to a month.

For a variation, omit the pumpkin seeds and replace with ½ cup of roasted unsalted peanuts or slivered almonds.

bick's muesli

Age: 12 months, plus

Keeps in an airtight container for 6 weeks

Makes: 6 cups

Prep time: 5 minutes

Cooking time: 1¼ hours

300 g rolled oats

50 g rice flakes

50 g barley

50 g triticale

50 g rye flakes

½ cup shredded coconut

½ cup sunflower seeds

½ cup slivered almonds

1–2 tablespoons honey

½ cup sultanas or dried cranberries
(or a mix of both)

Plain yoghurt and milk, to serve

My Dad, otherwise known as 'Bick' by his grandchildren, would have to be the best grandpa in the world. So hands on, so helpful and so clever at making muesli. Thanks, Dad, for all you do.

Preheat the oven to 100°C.

Combine all the ingredients, except the honey and dried fruit, in a large baking dish. Mix well.

Warm the honey in the microwave to soften and drizzle over the muesli mix. Stir. Bake in the oven for 1¼ hours, stirring every 15 minutes.

Remove and allow to cool. Either leave as is or whiz in a food processor if you want a finer texture. Mix in the dried fruit and store in an airtight container.

Serve with plain yoghurt and a small amount of milk.

tip You might need a trip to your local health food store to find all these ingredients but most supermarkets have them. If you can't find something, it's OK to leave it out. Alternatively, you can use a five-grain porridge mix that has all the oat and flakes. Simply use a combined quantity of 500 g. Remember that honey is not recommended for babies under the age of 1, due to the risk of infant botulism.

mexican pork and beans

Age: 12 months, plus

Suitable for freezing

Makes: 4 cups

Prep time: 15 minutes

Cooking time: 40 minutes

1 tablespoon olive oil

1 onion (100 g), diced

1 celery stick with stringy bits removed, diced

1 small carrot (100 g), peeled and diced

1 garlic clove, minced

1 teaspoon each ground cumin, ground coriander and dried oregano

250 g pork mince

200 ml salt-reduced chicken stock

2 tomatoes, peeled and diced

1 tablespoon tomato paste

½ red or yellow capsicum, deseeded and diced

⅓ cup medium-grain rice

1 × 300 g can red kidney beans or four-bean mix, drained and rinsed well

Although this could be just for your toddler, it makes a lovely fresh alternative to a well-known brand of Mexican dinners in a box for the rest of the family. This braise can be used as a filling for burritos or tacos with all the usual suspects, or as a stand-alone offering.

Heat the oil in a heavy-based saucepan with a lid and sauté the onion, celery and carrot for 5 minutes.

Add the garlic, herbs and spices and stir for 30 seconds until fragrant. Add the pork mince and brown for 3 minutes.

Add all the other ingredients and cook, covered, over low heat for 25–30 minutes, stirring occasionally. Season to taste.

Serve as is or with pieces of chopped cheese, tomato and avocado as finger food.

tip Try mashing the beans before they go into the pot.

panko prawns

Age: 12 months, plus (if egg-friendly)

Suitable for freezing

Makes: 1 serve

Prep time: 3 minutes

Cooking time: 3 minutes

1 tablespoon plain flour, for dusting

1 egg, lightly beaten

1 tablespoon Panko breadcrumbs (these are Japanese breadcrumbs, available in the Asian section of most supermarkets)

4 raw prawns per person, peeled and deveined, with tails left intact

1–2 tablespoons vegetable oil, for frying

People can't believe it when I tell them how much Louis loves prawns, but I guess lots of people don't think to offer their little ones prawn meat. Please do. Prawn flesh is delicious, soft and easy to chew. It's also versatile and makes a nice alternative to fish and chicken. You must use uncooked prawns for this recipe but it's easy to buy them frozen, peeled and deveined at most supermarkets.

Place the flour in a small bowl, the egg wash in another and the Panko breadcrumbs on a third plate. Place the prawns on absorbent kitchen paper to dry off. Dust each prawn in flour, holding it by the tail. Dip each prawn in the egg wash and cover it in Panko breadcrumbs, pressing down lightly. Set aside.

Cover the base of a frying pan with a thin film of oil and heat over medium heat until a breadcrumb starts to sizzle and brown when dropped into the pan. Place the prawns in the pan and cook for a couple of minutes on each side until golden-brown. Remove and drain on clean absorbent paper.

Serve with steamed veggies or Fried Rice (page 125). Sweet chilli is a great dipping sauce — it's sweeter than it is spicy.

Please note, shellfish can be a cause of allergies so test your baby on shellfish first, watching carefully for any reactions.

mee goreng

Age: 12 months, plus (if egg-friendly)

Not suitable for freezing

Makes: 1 serve

Prep time: 5 minutes

Cooking time: 5 minutes

50 g dried egg noodles

1 tablespoon vegetable oil

1 egg

¼ teaspoon minced garlic

¼ teaspoon minced or freshly
grated ginger

50 g chicken or pork mince
(or prawn meat)

¼ cup grated carrot

¼ cup finely shredded cabbage
or roughly chopped bean sprouts

1 chat potato, cooked, peeled
and diced

1 teaspoon kecap manis (sweet soy)

1 teaspoon tomato sauce

Stir-fried noodles are a great meal as you can get lots of veggies in there and either serve well chopped-up on a spoon or let your little one have a field day with a messy finger-food meal. Mee goreng is subtle in flavour, smooth in texture and a hit with all the family. If you're making some for the rest of the family, consider a touch of chilli sauce and white pepper to really finish off the dish.

Cook the noodles according to packet directions.

Heat half the oil in a large frying pan, add the egg and stir to lightly scramble. Remove and set aside. Heat the remaining oil and add the garlic, ginger and meat. Stir-fry for 1 minute.

Add the carrot, cabbage (or bean sprouts) and potato and stir-fry for 1 minute. Add the cooked noodles, the sauces and ¼ cup of water. Stir well until the liquid has mostly evaporated and the noodles are well coated with sauce.

Remove from the heat, stir through the scrambled egg and serve.

tip For an authentic touch, serve garnished with fried shallots (available at Asian grocers and some supermarkets).

avgolemono [greek lemon soup]

Age: 12 months, plus (if egg-friendly)

Not suitable for freezing

Makes: 2 serves

Prep time: 2 minutes

Cooking time: 12 minutes

500 ml salt-reduced chicken stock

2 chicken tenderloins

½ cup medium-grain rice

1 egg

1 teaspoon lemon juice

Chopped fresh parsley leaves

If you've never tried avgolemono, then do so. It's simple and delicious. This version has been tamed down for younger palates, but you'll get the idea.

Place the cold stock and chicken in a saucepan and bring to the boil. As soon as it's boiling, remove the chicken and set aside. Add the rice and cook for 12 minutes. Meanwhile, whisk the egg with the lemon juice and shred or finely dice the chicken.

When the rice is cooked, whisk the egg mix into the hot stock and return the meat to the pan.

Serve garnished with fresh parsley.

chicken fricassee

Age: 12 months, plus

Suitable for freezing

Makes: 2 cups

Prep time: 5 minutes

Cooking time: 20 minutes

1 tablespoon olive oil

1 onion (100 g), finely diced

1 garlic clove, minced

100 g mushrooms, finely chopped

1 quantity velouté (see below)

1 cup finely chopped cold roast chicken

1 tablespoon finely chopped fresh parsley leaves

Toast or cooked rice, to serve

Velouté ingredients

Velouté is essentially a white sauce but made with half stock/half milk to enhance the flavour.

3 teaspoons butter

3 teaspoons plain flour

125 ml salt-reduced chicken stock

125 ml full-fat milk

Fricassee is a French classic that, frankly, is not eaten enough by any of us. It's good, wholesome and super simple.

Heat a small frying pan over medium heat. Add the oil and sauté the onion for 10 minutes. Add the garlic and mushrooms and cook for a further 5 minutes.

Meanwhile, to make the velouté, place the butter and flour in a microwave-safe dish and microwave on high for 30 seconds. Add the stock and milk and whisk well. Microwave for 2 minutes. Whisk well. Microwave for a further 30 seconds to a minute, until thick.

Add the chicken, parsley and velouté to the onion mix and simmer for 5 minutes.

Serve with toast soldiers or cooked rice. Leftover fricassee can be frozen in portions.

tip Add finely diced carrots and peas along with the mushrooms to increase the veggie content.

dumplings

This is not a recipe, but more a suggestion. 'Dumpy Sunday' has become somewhat of a tradition in our house. It was one of our first shared meals as a family and we now all relish our Sunday dumpling lunches together.

Like many things, it came about as a bit of an accident. The whole family was sitting around the table, the babies with goodness knows what in their bowls, and John and I with a steaming plate of dumplings in between us. We all started to eat, but very quickly Sophie and Louis were way more interested in our chopsticks and dumplings than what they had. And surprisingly, or perhaps not, they loved them. And so a tradition was born. Now every Sunday we pull out the bamboo steamer, grab an array of dumplings from the freezer and 7 minutes later we all have a delicious lunch together.

Sweet soy, or kecap manis, is a favourite dipping sauce and it's also been known to help a few steamed veggies slide down at times.

Get down to your Asian grocer, buy a selection of frozen dumplings and start to have some fun with them. I was going to give you a recipe for dumplings but as I started developing it I decided not to bother. We are so lucky in Australia to have access to cheap, delicious and healthy food like this. I decided to take the easy option – after all, it's my weekend. And yours, too.

keftedes [greek meatballs]

Age: 12 months, plus (if egg-friendly)

Suitable for freezing

Makes: 15

Prep time: 5 minutes

Cooking time: 15 minutes

200 g beef mince

50 g (½) onion, finely diced

150 g potato, peeled and grated, moisture squeezed out

1 egg

1 tablespoon finely chopped fresh parsley leaves

Pinch each of ground cumin and cinnamon

½ teaspoon dried mint

Salt and pepper, to taste

1 tablespoon olive oil

My friend's Greek mum taught me how to make these and they are always a winner. I've simplified them a little to suit bubs, and oven-baked them not deep-fried them, but essentially they are as I was taught. Oh, so good.

Preheat the oven to 200°C. Line a baking tray with greaseproof paper.

Combine all the ingredients in a bowl and mix thoroughly, using your hands to really combine well.

Using a tablespoon, place dollops of the mixture on the oven tray and bake for 15 minutes.

Allow to cool before serving with yoghurt. I've also discovered a lemon and dill mayonnaise from the supermarket that makes a brilliant accompaniment.

prawn and cauliflower risotto

Age: 12 months, plus

Not suitable for freezing

Makes: 1 serve

Prep time: 5 minutes

Cooking time: 5 minutes

1 portion Risotto Base (page 101), about ¼ cup or to suit appetite

4 raw prawns, peeled and deveined, with tails left intact

1 tablespoon butter

¼ cup finely chopped cauliflower

Grated parmesan cheese

Chopped fresh parsley leaves

As babies get older they can become much fussier, especially with colour – some days it's all about green, the next orange, and so it goes. I created this risotto to be as colourless as possible and it's now one of our faves – Mum and Dad included!

Remove the Risotto Base from the freezer and thaw at room temperature or in the microwave.

Finely chop two of the prawns, reserving two for garnish (finger food) – or chop them all.

Heat the butter in a small saucepan and cook the whole prawns on both sides until their colour changes. Remove and set aside. Add the cauliflower and sauté for 2 minutes. Add the chopped prawn meat and stir until the colour changes. Add the risotto base and stir to combine until warmed through.

Stir in the cheese and serve sprinkled with fresh parsley.

banana ice cream

Age: 12 months, plus

Suitable for freezing

Makes: 1½ litres

Prep time: 5 minutes

Cooking time: 4 hours, minimum

1 litre vanilla ice cream

3 ripe bananas, peeled

Juice of half a lemon

Great for using up ageing bananas and great for giving your baby a rewarding second course that you know is packed with fruit. And it tastes just like a Barney Banana — remember those?

Leave the ice cream out of the freezer for 10 minutes to soften a little. Place the bananas in a food processor or blender. Add the ice cream and lemon juice. Pulse until well combined and the mixture is smooth.

Return to the ice cream tub or an appropriately sized container suitable for the freezer. Freeze until set and serve as required.

frozen strawberry yoghurt icy poles

Age: 18 months, plus (or whenever you feel your baby is ready for the cold blast)

Suitable for freezing

Makes: 6

Prep time: 5 minutes

Cooking time: 4 hours, minimum

1 punnet ripe strawberries, washed and hulls removed

3 tablespoons full-fat plain yoghurt

2 teaspoons castor sugar

1 teaspoon vanilla essence

To me, there is a romantic notion attached to homemade icy poles. I remember growing up and having flavoured ices made with fruit juice. The anticipation involved in setting up the moulds, adding the juice and then waiting for them to set was almost too much to bear. Our icy pole moulds are one of the favourite toys in the house and the excitement that erupts when they see them come out on a hot day in the backyard is something else. Be warned, these are best eaten in nappies only! You will need a food processor or blender for this recipe.

Set up the icy pole moulds. Whiz the fruit, sugar and vanilla for a few seconds until chopped and starting to go sloppy.

Add the yoghurt and whiz for another 30 seconds until well combined. Pour or spoon the mixture into moulds (or use ice cube trays and stick an icy pole stick in each one). Freeze and enjoy on a hot day.

For a variation on this recipe, you can make mango frozen yoghurts by following the recipe above and substituting mango flesh for the strawberries.

> tip Any leftovers can be stored in a freezer-safe container and enjoyed by mum and dad. Also, allow the icy poles to rest out of the freezer for a few minutes before giving to your toddler — gratification will be quicker.

meals for sick and recovering babies

It's heartbreaking watching your baby when he or she is sick. As a parent, all you want to do is make that nasty illness go away and nurse your baby back to health.

Unfortunately, it's not as easy as that. Sometimes there is not much we can do other than wait (especially in the case of gastro) and provide lots of small and regular feeds of appropriate meals:

Diarrhoea/gastro Go for clear fluids such as broth and lots of water. Include binding foods like ripe bananas and plain rice.

Constipation Prune juice will help to stimulate bowel function. High-fibre foods such as fresh pear puree and plenty of water will also help.

Fever Serve regular meals, but as feverish babies generally don't eat much add lots of butter and sauces to increase calories and ensure they drink plenty of fluids.

Sore throat Serve high-calorie ice cream and smoothies.

Stuffy nose Serve warm comfort foods such as soups.

Gentle first foods after colds and gastro-type illnesses include bananas (mashed and unsweetened), rice (plain white or rice flakes), apple puree (homemade with no sweetener) and plain toast.

Remember, please consult your health professional if you are concerned.

index

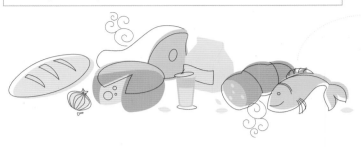